Masculine Emotional Intelligence

The 30 Day EI Mastery Program for a Healthy Relationship with Yourself, Your Partner, Friends, and Colleagues

John Adams

Dear Reader,

As an independent author,
  and one-man operation
  - my marketing budget is next to zero.

As such, the only way
  I can get my books in-front of valued customers
  is with reviews.

Unfortunately, I'm competing against authors and
  giant publishing companies
  with multi-million-dollar marketing teams.

These behemoths can afford
  to give away hundreds of free books
  to boost their ranking and success.

Which as much as I'd love to –
  I simply can't afford to do.

That's why your honest review
  will not only be invaluable to me,
  but also to other readers on Amazon.

Yours sincerely,

John Adams

Table of Contents

INTRODUCTION 7

CHAPTER ONE: HUMAN EMOTIONS 13

    HAPPINESS 14

    SADNESS 16

    FEAR 17

    DISGUST 19

    ANGER 19

    SURPRISE 21

    MORE ON EMOTIONS 23

CHAPTER TWO: THE EQ MODELS 43

    FIVE COMPONENTS OF EMOTIONAL INTELLIGENCE 45

CHAPTER THREE: BE AWARE OF YOURSELF 51

CHAPTER FOUR: REGULATE YOURSELF 63

CHAPTER FIVE: RECOGNIZING EMOTIONS 73

    RECOGNIZING EMOTIONS 76

    BODY LANGUAGE 78

CHAPTER SIX: SOCIAL SKILLS 88

CHAPTER SEVEN: 30 DAY EMOTIONAL INTELLIGENCE BOOSTER PROGRAM 97

    DAYS 1-5: GETTING TO KNOW YOURSELF 98

    DAYS 6-15: IMPROVING YOURSELF 104

    DAYS 16-21: EMPATHY 110

    DAYS 22-30: INFLUENCE 112

CONCLUSION 117

REFERENCES 123

Introduction

You are probably curious about emotional intelligence but still not sure about what it is, means, or looks like, then hold onto your hat because after this guide is through you will be able to understand what your emotional intelligence is and how to develop it.

Through the years, the importance of emotional intelligence has been widely recognized. In fact, one of the most famous books regarding emotional intelligence was published in 1995 by a man named Daniel Goleman. His book sought to help others understand what emotional intelligence (EQ) is. Goleman's work was largely influenced by the article that two psychologists published in an academic journal back in 1990. John Mayer and Peter Salovey laid the groundwork for what would lead to some of Goleman's greatest work.

It was not too long after this that emotional intelligence overtook the world and made its way into things such as children's toy advertisements and other conventional trade items. Since the days of Daniel Goleman's book, he has been impressed with how quickly emotional intelligence has been embraced by the general public as well as scholars.

So, what exactly is emotional intelligence and how does it affect you? The shorthand for emotional intelligence is EQ, and it stands for emotional quotient. Emotional quotient is just another name for emotional intelligence, so don't worry too much as the terms are interchangeable. You should get really familiar with this shorthand, because we are going to delve deep into the world of emotional intelligence. There are varying definitions explaining the boundaries and limits of EQ, but to put it in layman's terms, EQ is your ability to clearly distinguish and monitor your own personal emotions and the emotions of those that are around you. However, it is not this simple. Like everything in life, there are layers to your emotional intelligence.

Along with being able to control and realize your own emotions and the emotions of others, EQ involves the ability to identify the different types of emotions and accurately depict them. Per Goleman's description in his famous book, your EQ is also defined by the way that you process the information you have about emotions and use this emotional information to help guide the choices that you make, your own personal behavior, and how you influence others.

You might be wondering why EQ is so important. I am sure that all your life the importance of having a high IQ has been driven into your mind. But let's be honest. Success is more than just a high intelligence quotient. Having a high EQ is vital to your ability to succeed in life - in fact, the two go hand in hand with one another.

The list of reasons for why EQ is so pivotal to your success can span miles long, but to sum it up into two short and sweet points: your EQ relates to your own self-awareness and your social-awareness. These two categories can make or break a venture, and between you and me, I am sure you would rather be on the positive spectrum of this equation.

The main difference is that your IQ measures your cognitive intelligence. Your IQ is pretty easily measured through standardized testing. However, times have certainly changed in the last century and your IQ is not the only thing that matters anymore. With the understanding we have gathered on EQ, we now have several different branches of intelligence that go beyond the scope of the cognitive abilities we possess. For example, you might find that social intelligence overlaps a lot with emotional intelligence. Yet, it is extremely important to remember that they are two completely separate areas of intelligence and should not be interchanged with one another.

A growing number of businesses and employers are valuing EQ higher than they are IQ. Don't get me wrong, IQ is still a great thing to have and take pride in if you have a high one, but it is not a substitute for EQ. The game is changing. It has changed, and we were all asleep as EQ took over the world overnight.

In the job field, an overwhelming 71 percent of employers look at high EQ numbers versus high IQ numbers. Emotional intelligence is taking over the work force at an alarming rate, and there is a reason why. Those who have higher levels of EQ are reported to have increased job performance as well. This is why the mindset around EQ is shifting.

When surveyed in 2011, one in three managers reported that they would rather promote or hire a candidate that had higher EQ levels than one with higher IQ levels. The proof is in their work statistics. If a hiring manager thinks that your emotional intelligence is low, then they are far less likely to hire or promote you. According to 59 percent of managers that make the hiring decisions for their companies, low EQ means you're out.

In fact, if you are looking to move up into a position of leadership, then working on your emotional intelligence is the single best thing you can do to make sure that you stand out from your competitors. Why? It has been proven through research that managers with high EQ values have a significant decrease in team grievances - about an average of a twenty percent decrease! This is because they are able to read, understand, and adapt actions based on what they know about emotions. A boss or manager will look for all the qualities that signal someone is in tune with their emotional intelligence. They are watching to see if you can understand what emotions are on display, interpret them, and then react and respond accordingly. Nobody wins when there is a hothead in the office, or just an obtuse manager who will never understand why their staff is falling like flies.

The same can be said for relationships. When you bring high EQ values into a relationship, there is a larger chance for its success. That is because relationships are all about emotions! There are about 80,000 emotional calls that your partner sends out to you through the course of a forty year relationship. Being able to interpret and appropriately answer those emotional calls spells the difference between a relationship that is healthy and lasts and a relationship that fails.

If you find that you have problems in your career or your relationship, then you might want to examine your emotional intelligence before you do anything else. Regardless of how well you think you are doing, it is always a good idea to stop, take a breath, and figure out where your emotional intelligence lies.

I get it, I have been where you are too. Being reluctant is just a step in the process, but don't shelter yourself from information that can change your life. As men, we are often recalcitrant to make changes or to admit to the flaws that need to be worked on. But I am here to tell you that we can do better, and there is better for us. It just involves a little bit of self-work.

There are several reasons you might have picked this book up. Perhaps you wanted to learn more about emotional intelligence, or maybe you realized that you are lacking and need to get your emotional intelligence buffed up and ready for use. Whatever the reasoning, you need to know that you are not the only one of your kind - otherwise there would be no need for this book, now would there?

Your main problem is that you struggle to interpret the emotions of those around you and use them to help you navigate through work and love life situations. That stops today. I am looking forward to journeying through these next few chapters with you so that you can see what emotional intelligence is all about and how you can change your life with it.

If you have ever been passed up for a promotion or job that you felt you deserved, then delve right in. If you have been on the receiving end of a loved one telling you that you "just don't get it," then come on and start reading, because there will never be a better time than right now. Don't let another relationship or job pass you by before you decide to do something about it.

Being a man does not equate to having low emotional intelligence. Drive that line into your mind right now, because it is the truth. There are many powerful, successful men out there who are walking around in tune with their emotional intelligence. You could be one of them. Yes, being a man and conditioned to the world we live in, you might have to work a little harder to get your emotional intelligence to where you want it to be, but a little hard work never killed anyone.

You don't have to lack emotional intelligence. You don't have to lose relationships. You don't have to give up jobs and promotions. You can be your best self by simply understanding how your emotional intelligence works. I will be there with you through every step!

So, let us start by jumping head first into this problem, shall we? The first chapter is going to be all about emotions! We need to learn about them and talk about them if we are going to understand them. The next time your partner tells you that you "just don't understand," you'll be able to tell them that you do and safely navigate the emotional waters into your favor. If you are ready for your overall quality of life to improve, then what are you waiting for? Let's go find out more from those pesky emotions that constantly seem to elude us at our better moments.

Chapter One: Human Emotions

"There is no greater agony than bearing an untold story inside you." - Maya Angelou

Emotions can be difficult to understand and interpret, especially when the world we live in has left us without a base to understand them. Our emotions impact the way that we live, how we interact with those around us, what course of action we choose to take, as well as our understanding of our environment. So, where do we go in order to understand more about the emotions that seem to elude us? The main goal of this guide is to ensure you are able to master your masculine emotional intelligence. However, how can you reach that goal if you still don't understand what makes your EQ?

Luckily for us, the psychologists of our world have identified and landed on a basic set of emotions from which all other emotions build. While there are many different ideas and theories regarding emotions, there is still a base set of emotions from which the others are formed. This means that in order to begin understanding your EQ, you need to understand the emotions that you feel and that all others stem from.

It began with Paul Eckman who was a psychologist in the 1970's that decided upon and identified six "basic emotions" that everyone experienced through every culture. The basic emotions he coined were sadness, happiness, fear, surprise, disgust, and anger. While this list did later grow in order to include other feelings like shame, excitement, pride, and embarrassment, it is still agreed upon today that Eckman's base emotions are the foundation of other emotions.

However, the study of emotions did not stop with Eckman, and soon another psychologist named Robert Plutchik was giving his input about the world of emotions. In fact, Plutchik created the idea of a "wheel of emotions." This wheel was supposed to be just like the color wheel that we use. The emotions were combined or mixed to create other feelings. See? Just like you would mix green and yellow to get blue, you could mix anger and surprise to get another emotion. Eckman laid down the foundation for our basic emotions, but Plutchik brought forward the idea of combining these emotions into more complex emotions. It is important to remember, though, that all complex emotions stem from our list of basic emotions. They are the roots.

We have come a long way since the 1970's, and while Eckman's work is important for our foundation of understanding emotions, our understanding has grown far beyond what we knew in the 1970s. In 2017, a new study was released that showed that there are a lot more basic emotions than we first believed. The researchers published their work in the Proceedings of the National Academy of Sciences and indicated that they have found a total of twenty-seven other emotions. All these emotions occur on a scale, and rather than being distinct in their own right, each emotion is experienced on a gradient. They overlap with one another. However, in order to understand the gradient of emotions, we do need to take a more in depth look at the basic emotions that we will continue to build on for the rest of this guide.

Happiness

Happiness is one of the most common emotions that people want to experience. I mean, who does not want to be happy all the time? Or, perhaps, at least most of the time? The reason that happiness is such a sought after emotion is because it creates an emotional state that is pleasant for the person. We could all enjoy raised levels of contentment, satisfaction, gratification, and joy that promotes an overall healthier state of being. In fact, happiness is such an important emotional state that we humans try to achieve that the research rate has increased tenfold on it. From the 1960s and into today, a lot of branches within psychology study happiness and how to obtain it. One of the biggest areas of study within the happiness emotional state is "what does happy look like?"

I know that we all want to achieve happiness. We go to work, we live our lives, and maybe we start a family. But what does happiness look like within our ordinary lives? Happiness is expressed in several different ways that are crucial to look for in expanding your emotional intelligence (these will be further expanded on throughout the guide):

- Body language is key in understanding emotion. You will see most likely a relaxed position in the body.

- Facial expressions indicate emotional states first. Look for smiling and a relaxed face.

- Tone of voice can also indicate what emotional state a person is in. Happiness reflects in the voice in a normally upbeat tone.

Happiness does not look the same for everyone everywhere. This is important to remember, as cultural differences can severely impact what happiness looks like for someone. The different types of cultural experiences that a person subscribes to will influence what they stake as the parameters for their happiness. For example, in American pop culture today, it is believed that the path to happiness is paved with a house, a well paying job, a marriage, and maybe a child or two.

However, not all paths follow those directions to happiness. It is so important when you are considering emotional intelligence to understand that happiness impacts everyone differently. Happiness is a highly individualized emotion that does not always subscribe to what the next person thinks is happiness.

While happiness is a basic emotion, there is a strong correlation between happiness and physical health. It is no surprise that happiness is connected to mental health, but it can also impact how long your life is as well as any satisfaction or joy that is derived within a partnership (be that a friendship or a more intimate relationship). If happiness is linked to health, then being in a perpetual state of unhappiness is also linked to bad health. Diagnoses like depression, anxiety, and stress are highly linked to unhappy individuals. Understanding this is the key to understanding how to heighten your emotional intelligence.

Sadness

Another basic emotion is sadness. Sadness is normally characterized by feelings of disinterest, a low mood, and even grief. Sadness is a part of life, and as you know it is completely normal for people to experience sadness at intervals in life. When we miss a shot on a goal, or lose a game we were trying hard to win, it can feel defeating. It is important to be able to balance emotions. After all, we cannot be happy all the time.

A prolonged period of sadness can be debilitating and result in depression for the person who is experiencing the sadness. When you are looking for signs of sadness, you are normally looking for:

- A quietness within the subject

- Extreme lethargy; energy levels are below what they normally are

- If their mood seems sad, or upset

- If they begin to withdraw from everyone around them

- Tears and crying over the event that is causing sadness

Sadness occurs on a gradient, like all other emotions. Depending on what causes the sadness and how long the sadness goes on for, the severity of a bout of sadness can be debilitating. You want to be able to tell when sadness is triggering unhealthy behaviors in yourself and those around you. This way you can learn how to adapt and correct behavior. You want to repeat a positive series of actions to negate the feelings of sadness. This is not to say that you should try and never feel sad, but that you want to find healthy ways to cope with sadness experienced by you and others.

Fear

Fear is another basic emotion, but it plays a significant role in our lives — especially considering how powerful of an emotion fear is. So, why is fear so important? Throughout our lives we are going to be faced with a lot of different scenarios. Some of them are going to be ones that involve putting ourselves in danger or may even be life or death.

Fear results in what is known as the "flight or fight response." When you experience the fight or flight response, what happens is that your muscles will tense up and your breathing rate will increase. You might feel like your heart is pounding in your chest as well, but this is only as a result of an increased heart rate. Your mind will jump into overdrive as you examine every little thing in the scenario that has invoked fear within you. In these moments the fear is driving your mind to decide whether it wants to stay and fight the perceived danger, or whether you need to run as far away from the situation as possible. This response system is critical to your being able to decide how to manage threats that you feel. When trying to deduce what fear looks like you will see:

- eyes that widen, the chin being pulled back and other facial expressions pulled tight

- rapid breathing, an increased heart rate

- avoidance of the threat

Fear manifests differently in everyone. There are those of us who are more susceptible to fear and others who are harder to trigger. There are specific images and situations that can act as trigger warnings for us, and that manifests as the beginning of fear.

When presented with anything that your mind perceives as a threat, fear is going to be the first basic emotional response that is called to your body. As mentioned earlier, a gradient is the plane on which these basic emotions occur on and then expand into several other emotions. Why does this matter with fear? Well, fear can manifest in some particular detrimental behaviors when it exceeds the higher end of the fear gradient. For example, anxiety could be generated from the constant fear perpetuated in a person's mind. They then develop unhealthy fight or flight responses as a result of their anxiety.

Most people avoid situations that instill fear in them, however there are people that live off the adrenaline rush. These people seek out thrills that bring the rush of the flight or fight response. While fear can present as anxiety, it can also be adrenaline and create an excitement within the body.

Disgust

In Eckman's first basic emotions that he laid as the foundation, disgust was amongst the others. Disgust is the repulsion that a person feels toward another person, situation, or even an object. When you are looking for disgust as an emotion in either you or someone else, then you need to be watching the way that:

- their facial expressions manifest; they might wrinkle their nose or suppress the lines of their lips in disgust

- they turn away from what is causing disgust

- they physically react to the object of disgust; this might be vomiting or heaving in disgust

Disgust can be a direct result of multiple things, and as it occurs on a spectrum, like fear, disgust can be different for every person. A simple sight, smell, sound, or even taste could end up being the trigger for a person. Throughout history it is believed that this emotion developed as a reaction to stay away from bad or dangerous foods and situations. However, as time has progressed, so has the scale of disgust.

Anger

Anger is among the basic six emotions that all other emotions were founded on. It is a powerful emotion, one that is based on frustration, hostility, and agitation. Anger is normally manifested from an act or event, and can even be the result of a perceived threat. We all react differently to various stimuli, so what might strike fear in one man strikes anger in another. When you are looking for signs of anger, look for:

- yelling or harsh tones in their voice

- frowning of the lips, glaring, or hard glaring with the eyes

- strong body language, closed off stance or even moving away from a person

- behavior that is physically aggressive where there are broken objects, hitting, or even kicking of objects

- turning red in the face, sweating from stress and anger

Anger is normally termed as a negative feeling or emotion, however when let off in the right way it can be a healthy and constructive emotion. I am sure you have heard the term "blow off some steam." That is normally used when expressing the need to let some anger out in a healthy manner. The reason it is important to let your anger out in a healthy manner is because it can afford you some clarity that you need to navigate relationships and carry out certain actions.

Like all things, anger can become a detrimental emotional problem. If a person does not learn how to control their anger using healthy outlets, then their behavior can become abusive and dangerous to those in relationships with them or to those who just so happen to find themselves in the angry person's path on a bad day. Because anger is such a delicate emotion when not handled correctly, it can spiral into a huge problem that creates both physical and mental consequences for all those involved. When your anger controls you, there is very little control that you have over making sound decisions.

Surprise

The final emotion that forms the foundation of the basic six emotions is surprise! If you have ever had a present, a birthday, or lived long enough on this planet to cognitively process information, then you have most likely dealt with the emotion of surprise. Surprise is an emotion that is never long term, but rather brief in nature.

Surprise is one of the basic emotions that can take hold in several different ways. It does not have to be positive every time or negative every time. Surprise can manifest either positively or negatively depending on how a person has received the information regarding the surprise. For example, a good surprise for some of us might be getting new golf clubs on our birthdays — or even just because. A bad surprise might be finding out that the leftovers you were looking forward to eating all night were cleared out before you managed to even have another bite. When trying to identify what surprise looks like, look out for:

- any physical response such as jumping, hand clapping, or shaking.

- subtle or not so subtle facial expressions such as widened eyes, a gasping mouth, and even raised brows.

- any verbal response that includes screaming, yelling, or even a gasp

Similar to fear and anger, your fight or flight response can be triggered when you are placed in the emotional state of surprise. This is because you can become startled and the adrenaline associated with the fight or flight response is generated within your body. Surprise can be used when we are making quick and minute responses to stimuli in our environment.

So, that is the breakdown on what the six basic emotions are, what to look out for in order to discern them from one another, and how they can affect the body and mind. Humans are emotional creatures. As much as the world would like to discount the emotions of men, we too are emotional beings. While we might like to think that all of our decisions are based on fact and logic, that is not true. In fact, it is farthest from the truth. Our every decision is based on the emotions that we feel and experience. These emotional triggers become the way that we process our actions and decisions. Our bodies end up building a standard set of reactions that we revert to when exposed to those emotions.

When I was younger and still learning a lot about emotional intelligence, I did not realize just how important my emotions were in every fundamental decision I ever made. One of the most distinct memories I have is when I got incredibly angry at a slight that I believed a friend had done against me. This friend we will call Mark. After fifteen years of friendship, going through the ups and downs, we had a disagreement at lunch over a topic that I held near and dear to my heart. Because this topic meant so much to me, my judgement was clouded and I was closed off to all other perspectives that did not align with mine.

Yes, I had research, facts, and figures to back up my position. I thought I was entirely logical in my thought responses. I got so angry that I shut him off and I turned away from the friendship. Out of anger. I let my anger control my decision and I made a very rash choice in the heat of the moment. Of course, I soon realized that I was not being logical in the decision to end the friendship. I have learned a lot about emotional intelligence through the years and I have expanded on my own levels of EQ. Because of this, I am able to better control my actions in every single one of my emotionally charged states.

More on Emotions

It became very clear that more than just the six basic emotions existed. When Eckman first began his research, he classified that the six emotions he laid as the foundation to all other emotions were experienced by all humans across all cultures. However, these theories adapt and change as we learn new information and are provided with new facts. Eckman added a series of other emotions to his foundational list as he continued to study emotions more in depth throughout the rest of his career.

There is a key difference in the following emotions that Eckman added on versus his original six basic emotions. His basic emotions relied on tell-tale physical and facial cues to interpret, however these newly added emotions were not necessarily given away by any facial cues or physical actions. These new emotions that Eckman expanded his list with were:

- Excitement

- Relief

- Contentment

- Amusement

- Satisfaction

- Guilt

- Pride

- Embarrassment

- Shame

Now, remember that there are many great minds in this world, and not all great minds think alike or agree on theories - particularly those theories that are based on emotion. Eckman's research was groundbreaking and important to the study of emotions, but it is important to know that not all theories and psychologists agreed with Eckman's classifications of emotions. There are many other theories out there regarding how our emotional state affects our human experience.

These theories are as vastly different as they are numerous in quantity. There are theorists who believe that only three basic emotions exist to make up the foundation for all other emotions. Some researchers believe that emotions occur in a form of hierarchy. Your top emotions would be those such as love, anger, sadness, joy, and surprise. Secondary emotions are broken down from the top emotions experienced. For example, from love we can then get affection and tenderness. It does not stop here though, as they continue to break down these secondary emotions into a third tier. So, you might have love first, then you have affection and tenderness, and from that you find emotions like compassion and care for others.

As I mentioned above, the latest research that is most widely believed across the psychological field is that twenty-seven different emotions exist and connect to one another on a gradient.

The researchers that tested these emotions used a group of 800 men to study and control. They had these 800 men watch over 2,000 videos — each video designed to prompt an emotional response from the viewer. The researchers examined and notated every single emotional response that these men had to the stimuli presented toward them. This was largely in an effort to understand how each emotion related to the other.

Dacher Keltner was the senior researcher for this study. He works for the Greater Good Science Center as their faculty director. However, it was not just him alone. A team of researchers came together and found that they could identify twenty-seven emotions that were distinct from one another in the responses given by the men.

So, based off of this new information that they compiled from the men, it was easy to deduce that emotions are not singular feelings that happen one at a time per the stimuli presented, but that they can occur on a gradient. Each emotion that was felt was connected to the next, rather than separated as was first suggested back in the 1960s.

Emotions are important to study because they not only affect our moods, but they affect our behaviors, our physical conditions, and our mental states. In fact, it is heavily emphasized that the more we can identify our emotions, the easier we make the research for everyone invested in understanding not just the human mind and psyche but also the human body.

Your emotions influence your everyday life, whether you are ready to admit it yet or not. We are not beings that run on logic and operate from learned placed. Instead, we are governed by our emotions in everything that we do. The way that we interact with others and our environment is all pre-determined by our emotions. You want to be able to understand these emotions that you are experiencing, because the direct result will be that you will have gained deeper insight and control over your actions.

Your emotions are as complicated as you are as a person — and if you want to say that you are not complicated, let me get ahead of you right here. Humans are all complex creatures. Every single one of us has a complex body with an even harder to understand mind to accompany it. We are confusing creatures at the best of times. However, this does not mean that you do not have a chance at understanding and controlling that complexity. All of your emotions work together on a gradient to express your feelings about the stimuli in your environment, and when you can understand that, then you are already halfway to understanding how to have greater control over your emotional responses and actions.

Your emotions are divided into two very distinct groups that have survived for decades — basic emotions and complex emotions. Your basic emotions are standard emotions that can be foundational for other emotions and are easy to identify as they have set appearances and facial expressions to accompany each feeling. You already know that sadness, happiness, fear, anger, disgust, and surprise comprise some of the basic emotions we experience. So, it becomes easy to tell when someone is happy because they are smiling happily and their stance is open and receptive throughout communication.

Complex emotions can be harder to read because their cues can be made up of several components that are interchangeable amongst other emotions. Yes, while the basic emotions are usually a lot easier to tell apart from one another, the lines between them can also become blurred. This is because a person's body language or facial cues are not always accurate representations of the emotion that they are feeling.

We have learned and adapted to not always show our true emotions on our faces. Why? Because there are moments when we want to hide our true feelings from those around use for a myriad of reasons. For example, if you are having a family dinner but received particularly unsettling news right before dinner, you might still put a smile on your face and be perceived as cheerful. You do this for several reasons, but in the end you have managed to mask your true emotional response to your stimuli.

However, there are also times when your emotional response might not be easily understood even when you want it to be. This is because emotions can manifest themselves in several ways across a person's body and face. For example, when a person is depressed, their face might take on the cues that are more closely associated with anger. A regular feeling of sadness will be quite distinct from the facial cues that are seen with depression. Do you see how this can become tricky?

Remember, just because we call it a basic emotion does not mean that emotion cannot be broken down into more categories. Earlier I mentioned how surprise can manifest both as a negative or positive emotion. It is key to understanding your EQ to also understand that even the basic emotions can be complex when we are learning about them. Basic simply means the foundation or the first, not basic in terms of simplicity.

Emotions can vary depending on the person that is expressing them. This is because across different cultures and experiences, there are different ways that people learn to use their emotions in response to their environment. For example, everyone goes through and processes their grief in a different way. For some people, anger is a completely normal stage to grief. They might find that they need to let their anger about the loss out before they can move on and experience a different range of emotions. For others, anger might never come into play with their loss.

Grief is one of those complex emotions that we keep talking about. There is still argument about all the different emotions that are comprised within grief, but the general consensus agrees that surprise, fear, anger, denial, sadness, and acceptance are all components within grief. While they are separate emotions, a person will go through each one on a gradient and each emotion will be connected to the last in order to form the complex emotion of grief. There is no one simple way to understand these emotions, because like I keep saying they vary from person to person. This is important to your EQ, because you need to learn to understand your emotions and your response to situations. Then you need to always remember that not everyone is going to have the same response that you do to your environment.

Your emotions can begin to affect your health and your personality when they are sustained over a long period of time. Let us continue examining grief for this example. Since grief is made up of many different emotions that are experienced over a period of time, the emotional stage of grief can last for some time. When we experience a certain emotion for a prolonged period we then find that we have changes in our thought processes and our behaviors.

Why Do We Have Emotions?

So, now that you understand more about the basic components of emotions, how emotions function, and where they come from, why do we have them? Your emotions are a necessary part of your everyday life. They help you navigate the different situations that you encounter. This is why EQ has become so prevalent and overtaken the importance of IQ, because your EQ gives you the ability to understand what emotional response and action is appropriate in the moment.

Psychological issues and mental illness are the direct result of an overflow of emotion. I am not just talking about the big disorders like depression, but also the lesser publicized problems like phobias, obsessive disorders, anxiety, borderline personality disorder, substance abuse, and traumas (PTSD included). On the spectrum of emotions, as humans, we feel everything. Sometimes this can feel like a real kick in the butt to have to constantly deal with our emotions, but there is a power to it once you understand how to handle your emotions.

Emotions are the reason for our survival. If it wasn't for our emotions, our bodies would be at a loss about how to respond to situations and environmental stimuli. For example, if we did not have the emotion of fear, we would probably fail at recognizing when we need to flee a dangerous situation. If you were to ever come face to face with a polar bear and your emotional fear system did not respond, you would most likely end up mauled before you had a chance to logically process the situation. Your emotions are akin to your first system of response.

You could make the argument that there are many natural things that exist in this world that do not rely on emotion. So, again, why do humans have such an intrinsic emotional response built into our systems? It exceeds our need to survive in the world. If we only needed to survive, then all we would need are emotions that bring our adrenaline up and our fight or flight response to the table. The reality is that humans are complex and emotional creatures. Our lives revolve around more than just instinct, and we live for more than just the need to survive. Our basic emotions help us navigate and survive the world, but our more complex emotions allow us the ability to interact with and envision our world or our place in the world.

As the world has modernized and changed, so too have our emotions adapted to assist us in living and dealing with the new stimuli that we face every day. A roaming polar bear is less of a fear, but impending debt, a new job interview, or even that first date could be enough to jerk our fight or flight response into high gear. I mentioned before that mental illness is an excess of emotion within a person that goes uncontrolled. This is true, and it can have devastating effects on the way that a person acts and the choices that they make with their environment.

In short, our emotions are very important to our daily functioning, our reasoning, as well as our relationships — this includes work and intimate relationships. However, when emotion plays such a large role in our daily lives, it becomes hard to discern when we are doing a good job at controlling it or not, particularly when a certain emotion becomes excessively felt and displayed. For example, when we live in a constant state of fear that turns into an anxiety that we live with, this can hinder our work life and our romantic life. So, therapy emerges with different tactics and procedures that one can implement in their lives to try and regain and maintain balance in their emotional life. The use of therapy assists us with making sure that we can step back from our overwhelming emotions and rationalize them so that we can make the right decisions.

In today's function, emotion serves the purpose of helping us relate to the community around us and to continue to build a farther reaching community. Nobody wants to be closed off or uncaring about the world around them, and if you find yourself in that position, then you likely have an unbalanced emotional feeling within you. Life is hard, and it can be harder when we are faced with navigating through different relationships with people. At our core, it is our emotions that allow us to connect to our world, and we should never take that for granted. In the next few sections, we are going to take a closer look at emotions and list all the ways that they help us, as this is ultimately why we need emotions.

- Emotions enable us to avoid dangerous situations as well as thrive in our environment. The study of emotions can date back to the time of Charles Darwin, who believed that in order to survive, our emotions are an adaptation that came around. Our emotions adapted from a need that humans were lacking, and now they have response systems to stimuli in their environment that help them navigate the world's sticky situations. They help us learn what we want to positively seek out and what we want to avoid. Our avoidance would be for the negative experiences. So, when faced with a lion, we might change paths and run away, but when faced with the prospect of feeling cared for in a prospective mate, our positive emotional experience will allow us to connect with the other person.

- Emotions are decision makers. Every choice that we make, every fork that we choose to go down in life, is fueled by an emotion. In fact, even the decisions you might think have no emotion behind them are fueled by emotion — a decision as small as what to have for breakfast. I promise you that even the most logical man has his emotions fuel his decisions. If you are shaking your head no to my previous statement right now - that's an emotional response.

- Our emotions allow us to connect with others and allow others to understand us better. It can be hard for other people to see into our lives and our minds sometimes, and that is where emotions play another major role. The emotions that we express give the people we are interacting with insight into our feelings and emotional state of mind. Through our facial expressions and our body language we give off cues about our emotions to others. Sometimes we are experts at masking our true feelings, but we can also allow others insight into our feelings. We can verbally communicate to others what we are feeling by directly telling them. They use this information in order to make their decisions on how to interact with us.

- Emotions also allow us to understand the emotional state of those that we are interacting with. That's the great thing about emotions; they are not just a one way street. We can read their emotions and interpret them, the same way that we allow them to do for us. When we take a moment to examine the world around us, we are able to gather information about our social standing with others as well as their emotions. Understanding how to appropriately navigate social communication impacts the way that we communicate with others and how successful we are at it. Responding in the right way to other people is essential because it is the pathway to building deeper relationships, strengthening existing relationships, and connecting with others on an emotional and social level. Connection is the greatest tool that we have in our human arsenal, and we should take every advantage that we can in order to use it for our benefit. The other benefit of being able to read and interpret emotions and social communication is that we benefit from it in the workplace.

From this chapter, you should now really understand why we need emotions to function and why they are so important to us as humans. Emotions were not given to us by a happy accident, but they are a necessary adaptation that we need in order to survive. With that being said, emotions are still complex ideas that we need to try our best to understand in order to navigate their waters accurately.

Emotions are tools that we need to know how to handle, because like other weapons and tools, when we do not know how to control them, they can become dangerous. But they bridge divides between people, between nations, and even between cultures. Emotions are the epitome of human communication.

How Do Emotions Fool Us As Men?

If emotions are the epitome of human communication, what does that mean for us as men? You have probably grown up your entire life being told that you are not a good emotional communicator, or that you should even mask your emotions because feeling and displaying emotions as a man was not an appropriate response.

It's not surprising that there are a host of men out there that exist who have trouble explaining or expressing their feelings to those around them, particularly when they enter into romantic and personal relationships. Emotions can be tricky fields for men to navigate, because we have been taught that we should not feel, that part of our manly existence is to be nonchalant about what happens to us and around us. Raising our EQ is fundamental to our success as men in any part of our life.

As a man, you need to work to break the boundaries that have been imposed on you and that you have been raised with. You need to destroy the stereotype of the emotionless man that society has tried to put on you over the course of your entire life. This will take active work by you in order to make sure that you are constantly and consistently expressing your emotions to the ones that you care about. Being vulnerable with your emotions is not something that you should be afraid of. Instead, it should be something that you embrace. When you accept your emotions and become ready to share them, you begin to raise your EQ.

The first step can just be admitting your emotions to yourself. Sometimes, this is the hardest. Nobody wants to admit when their feelings overwhelm them or when they are feeling an emotion that strays away from the "macho" emotions that are considered appropriate to show. It can help to take small steps. When you wake up in the morning, repeat a mantra to yourself in the mirror or even have it written on notes hung around your house. It should be a mantra that is about your emotions, a positive admission of how you are feeling and that you are entitled to that feeling. It can be as simple as "Today I am angry" or "Today I feel sad." Your emotions are your power, and you should not be afraid to express the way that you feel.

Emotions are tricky for men, because we shut them off for so long that we forget what to look for when others are exhibiting concerning emotions. We lose our ability to properly react to their responses. We need to accept what we feel as men in order to embrace the emotions of others and have others embrace our emotions.

There are two main emotions that men experience. These are happiness and anger (I promise you being horny is not an emotional state, so don't try to add that one in, it will not garner as much sympathy as you think). I myself have had problems embracing my own emotions. This is because of the way that society has drilled into me that as a man, I should have none.

When I came to realize that I was avoiding all of my emotions that I thought were not "macho" enough, it was the first step that I needed to start accepting every single one of my emotions. Anger can be a hard emotion for men to master because of the unhealthy relationship that we have with it. We have been taught that anger is the only safe, rational emotion for a man, and that it is normal to find ourselves angry. We are also taught that there is a delicate balance with angry, and being too angry and too emotional is a bad thing as well.

When we respond to our emotions, we are succumbing to one of two possible response types. There is the primary response and the secondary response. Your primary emotion is simply your first emotional response, the one that you automatically feel when stimuli in your environment affects you.

Secondary emotion is our second round of emotional response. This occurs when we are hard on our emotions and the way that we feel about things. Instead of our primary response to the stimuli, we hide our feelings and mask it with our secondary emotional response. This can cause issues and a lack of comfort for the person who is masking their true feelings.

It can be very difficult trying to reprogram the way that you have been brought up to hide and destroy your primary emotional response. I had a friend whose childhood and adolescence were especially hard on him. His family never accepted when he was sad, and anytime he displayed the emotion he was promptly chastised and ignored. In fact, he was told to "be a man about it" and "man up" when it came to his emotions. So, whenever he felt sad or an emotion that his family deemed was not manly, he learned to replace it with anger to hide his vulnerability and protect himself.

This hindered his future relationships, because when my friend finally got married, his partner was quickly fed up with his anger and his bluntness that was a result of his anger. His marriage suffered pretty quickly because he was unable to display any affection that was not seen as manly, or at least that he did not perceive as manly. My friend constantly complained that his marriage made him feel angry and that it was in a bad state, but he had no idea how to change the state of his marriage.

At first, I did not think much of this, but after a while of him telling me about his anger I asked him if he ever felt sad about his marriage. He broke down eventually and described his emotional turmoil that he kept hidden inside and masked so that he never displayed weakness. It was not long before my friend shut himself down and admonished himself for being open and vulnerable. His anger came back out and kicked the sadness to the curb.

This inability to connect with his sadness stemmed from the way that his parents brought him up and drilled within him that he could never feel anything that was not appropriate for a "man" to feel. But, his admission of sadness was the step in the right direction. Slowly and surely his wife began to understand him a little bit more.

You see, our responses of anger are designed so that we can protect ourselves from feeling any other emotion that might hurt or damage us. The object is to avoid pain and to let the anger take control.

So, why is it so hard to put aside our secondary emotional response and allow our real emotion to show through? The reason is that it can be scary to open yourself up raw to a partner and trust them not to pick apart at your delicate emotions. The problem begins when we continually shield our true emotions with anger. We become the root cause of all emotional distance within a relationship. We would rather yell and get mad because this is deemed as the correct male response than cry or admit vulnerability in our emotions. Nobody wants to be seen as weak, so we will curl away from emotions that we have been taught are weak emotions. In this regard, society and our upbringing have really let us down.

To be truly strong, you need to be able to fully express your emotions. This includes the full range of your emotional capabilities, and not just the emotions that are seen as "macho" or strong. As soon as my friend admitted to himself and his wife how much time and energy he spent trying to mask his emotions, they began to see a real change in their relationship. He began to open himself up to his wife and allow her to see parts of him that he had never shown her before.

Your emotions have a direct correlation with your partnership and how happy both you and your partner will be due to your feelings. When you hide them, you are effectively shutting your partner out and creating a wall that exists between the two of you.

Childhood behaviors can be hard to break or shake as we grow older. This is because it is like a bone that has grown out of shape and needs constant work to slowly pull it back into the correct place.

Behaviors are not easy to change once they are set in, however, we should always try and make positive changes when it comes to our emotions. The benefits you get when you embrace your emotions will be immediate and you will forever be grateful. If you want to connect with those around you, then you need to be able to be open about your emotions.

In intimate relationships, being honest about your feelings is the only true way to make the relationship real and to make it work. When in a fight with your partner, instead of being angry or using your anger as a deflection for your other emotions, be honest. Tell your partner "This is hurting me, I am sad" or even "Us fighting like this disappoints me." You will be able to reach them on a similar emotional level, you will meet each other halfway, and the fight will soon be a distant memory as you guys work together through your emotions to fix the problem. Your anger does nothing but escalate an already tense situation, especially when pride comes into the picture. Put these weapons down when communicating through tense situations. They don't help your progress the same way that emotional honesty will.

I know it can be tempting to fall into the stereotype of the man who feels nothing, but you will harm every relationship that you ever have with this train of thought. Despite our best attempts as labelling men as unfeeling, this is not true. We are human beings. We feel every range of emotion that our opposite gender feels. We have just been systematically brought up to repress those feelings. So, instead of being in tune with how we feel, our emotions are foreigners to us and they trick us because we do not get to know them. Our society has left men at a distinct disadvantage as it has undermined our ability to feel and embrace our emotions. This is a disadvantage that I seek to correct!

Whoever said that you cannot teach an old dog new tricks has never tried to show a man how to access his true emotions. It is entirely possible for you — no matter what your age is — to tap into the emotions that you have locked away. Hopefully, by correcting this problem now, we can spare an entire generation of men from having to battle with embracing their emotions.

Yes, men might have a harder time because of societal norms expressing how they truly feel. However, this does not mean that they do not feel their emotions. They do, and they feel them deeply. They are just forced to suppress these emotions and because of that their emotions become strangers to them. They are unsure of how they feel and why, and they revert to the automatic response of anger.

Emotions that men feel may be mistaken for others. When we feel sad or even vulnerable we will override them with pride and anger in an attempt to seem "macho." Do you see how this macho man stereotype is doing a disservice to our entire gender? We need to throw aside the antiquated societal conventions about men and their emotions and learn what our emotions are really telling us and how they are making us feel.

There are so many instances in your life as a man that will require you to rely on your emotions — the emotions that don't include anger or pride. You will likely take on the roles of colleague, lover, partner, husband, dad, grandad, and so on. All of these roles will at some stage require you to tap into what you are truly feeling in order to make real connections and progression.

I had a friend named Jim, and he came to me with a serious problem. His youngest daughter had been seriously and physically harmed by a boyfriend of hers. His reaction to the event alienated both his wife and his daughter, as he only let his anger surface and he focused on wanting to hurt the boyfriend. His family was in serious distress over his words and they were fearful that if he carried out his threat that he would find himself arrested. Jim's anger was a cover up for how he truly felt, but he was unable to understand or work through his real emotions, so he expressed himself in anger.

Together, Jim and I got him some help and we talked through his emotions. We found that at the root of his feelings he was deeply sad and tormented that he could not help his daughter's pain. He felt like he was at fault for all that his daughter had gone through, that he had somehow fundamentally failed her. Here is the turning point in Jim's story. He was finally able to confront his true emotions, and be honest with himself and his family. He did not need to exact revenge on the boyfriend, but to be honest with his family and himself and help his daughter heal and move forward.

This is not an isolated story, either. There are thousands upon thousands of men out in the world today who struggle with the same concept of being true with their feelings. They are fearful of society's backlash if they express their true emotions, and therefore they leave themselves at a large disadvantage.

We need to change society's perception of men dealing with their emotions in healthy and positive ways. We can not expect men to do better and show emotion when we are systematically cutting them down for doing that very same thing.

We deserve the same chance and ability as women have at understanding and embracing our emotions. Emotions should not be foreigners to us that end up tricking us or fooling us into situations that are far worse than if we had just been honest about our true emotions in the first place. Now, more than ever, when EQ is such an important value in the workplace and at home, it is essential that we educate and help other men around us boost their EQ and understand that their emotions are not something to be afraid of expressing.

I could give you an endless amount of examples where men have struggled to express themselves with the people in their lives. There are also often defining moments when their emotions come to the surface and shock those around them because it is unusual for them to fully express themselves. Men experience emotions on the same intensity that women do, we have just failed men by not equipping them with the same practice and expertise that women have in dealing with emotions. Their only options are to bury their emotions deeper and overlap them with macho emotions like anger and pride.

It is easy to see that men are not creatures that do not feel and have no emotion. Rather, they are humans who society has trapped in a shell where they are unable to be hurt, cry, or be sad because then they are too effeminate and not manly enough if they actually express these emotions. That shell needs to be broken, and that is what we are going to work on through this guide.

Chapter Two: The EQ Models

"Human behavior flows from three sources: desire, emotion, and knowledge." - Plato

There have been so many researchers that have studied emotional intelligence, from Peter Salovey and John Mayer to David Goleman and even more recent researchers who understand the importance of EQ. Through their research they have come up with three models that are used in the field of understanding and representing emotional intelligence. The models that are widely used are:

- The Trait Model

- The Ability Model

- The Mixed Model

The model that we will refer to in this guide is David Goleman's mixed model, as it is the most universally used model. But, we will also expand on and explain the other models that we will use or reference in this guide.

The Ability Model

The ability model was created by Peter Salovey and John Mayer. It was the first of the models to be created and used to understand EQ. The Ability Model follows the following outline:

- Perceiving emotions: this is where we can understand nonverbal communication and signals such as body language and facial expressions.

- Reasoning with emotions: this is where we use our emotions in positive ways to conduct our thinking and our decision making processes. Our cognitive activity is used during this step.

- Understanding emotions: we need to understand and interpret the emotions of those that are around us. When we can tell if people are angry, sad, or hurt and what is causing their emotions i.e.: are you the cause or is a particular situation the cause of their emotions?

- Managing emotions: the final process of the ability model includes the ability to regulate and control your emotions and respond with the appropriate emotions to situations every single time.

The Mixed Model

David Goleman makes use of what he calls "The Five Components" in his mixed model. His attempt to describe emotional intelligence makes use of the components in his model below:

- Self-Awareness includes your confidence and the ability to recognize feelings.

- Self-regulation includes your ability to control your emotions, your trusting of your emotions and your adaptability.

- Motivation is your drive, commitment, optimism, and initiative

- Empathy is your ability to understand the feelings that others have, your attention to diversity and even your political awareness.

- Social skills is the final arc in this model where your leadership skills, conflict management, and communication skills are on display.

The Trait Model

The trait model was created by Konstantin Vasily Petrides, and he himself called the trait model a constellation in which your emotional perceptions of yourself are found at the lowest levels of personality. His description of emotional intelligence involves two points:

- Your understanding and perception of your own emotions

- Using the framework of your personality to understand and investigate emotional intelligence based on personality traits.

Five Components of Emotional Intelligence

Emotions come in a gradient where there is a wide variety of different emotions that a person can feel at any point in time. The great thing about emotions is that normally there are behaviors exhibited when a person is feeling a certain emotion that can be observed and recorded. Your emotions include your behavior (like body language and facial expressions), the feelings that you express, and any changes in your state of mind. Each individual will feel their emotions differently, and the way that we express them is what gives our personalities their individuality. Intelligence comes into play with our emotions by the way that we can learn about emotions and then apply that learned behavior. Essentially, emotional intelligence is just your ability to manage other people successfully based on what you know about their emotions. You do need to understand your own feelings first in order to understand those of other people that you interact with. Daniel Goleman has already given us the five components that make up emotional intelligence. To go over them once more, they are:

- Self-Awareness

- Self-Regulation

- Motivation

- Empathy

- Social Skills

Self-Awareness

Self-awareness if your ability to first realize your own emotions, motivations, and then abilities. After you realize these, you also need to be able to understand them. It includes not just understanding your moods, but also understanding how your moods affect those that are around you. Goleman believes that when you are in a place of total self-awareness, you are controlling your emotional state and identifying every emotion that you feel. These are the traits you can work on and look for in others to see if they are mature enough emotionally to be self-aware:

- the ability to laugh at your own mistakes or goofs

- confidence in yourself

- being aware of how others see you

Self-Regulation

Being able to control your actions and first hand impulses is incredibly important when you are dealing with emotions. Often, we want to lash out with the first emotion we feel, but if we are truly self-aware then we are able to process these emotions and identify the appropriate emotion to react with. In essence, this is your ability to think before you react or say anything about a situation. Through self-regulation, you are emotionally mature when you are able to:

- be responsible for your own actions

- adapt to changes in the environment

- respond correctly to the irrational behaviors or emotional displays of others

That last one can be very hard to do, especially in an emotionally charged situation. For example, when someone is yelling and screaming at you, it can be tempting to yell and scream back. But being emotionally mature means that you are able to stop, interpret what they are truly mad at, and then approach the situation with the right emotion. A person who self-regulates well would not feel the need to yell back automatically.

Motivation

Your motivation is actually one of the most, if not the most, crucial components in emotional intelligence. Motivation is how interested you are in learning about emotions and your own self-improvement. You need to be motivated to jump over the hurdles and obstacles you will face or you will get nowhere if you have no drive. When you are motivated, you will set goals for yourself and you will follow through and hold yourself accountable for them (yes, this does also tie into self-regulation). The traits you display when you are motivated are:

- taking initiative

- showing commitment to the completion of a task

- persevering even when adversity is mounting high against you

Feeling motivated all the time can be hard to accomplish and frustrating when you feel like you fell short of your goals. Keep in mind that you do not have to be 100 percent successful all of the time. For example, when you choose to motivate yourself with smaller goals that are meant to help you become a better person or a more knowledgeable person, then you are practicing internal motivation and that is a sign of being emotionally mature. Exterior motivations are where you seek to attain riches and wealth or a position of power for the benefit of looking good to those around you - this is emotionally immature behavior and not a good basis for motivating yourself.

Empathy

Empathy is your ability to interpret the emotions and reactions of other people around you. You are not going to succeed at being empathetic if you are not self-aware. All of these components interconnect with one another, and you cannot achieve a high emotional intelligence without each component. Goleman's belief is that you need to have a fundamental understanding of yourself and your emotions before you can try and understand others. When you emulate empathy while being emotionally mature it looks like:

- being perceptive of others' feelings and actions

- having a true interest in the problems and concerns of other people

- having the ability to understand and anticipate another person's emotions regarding a situation or problem

- being aware and understanding societal norms and the actions of people.

For example, when you are truly empathetic, you can understand the feelings that someone else is going through, particularly feelings of sadness or hurt. You do need to understand yourself completely and have a good grasp on your own feelings before you can understand people who differ from you and your experiences.

Social Skills

The final component is your social skills. Social skills include a vast range of abilities and interactions but they are mainly your ability to understand sarcasm, jokes and innuendos around you, your customer service, and your ability to hold on to and maintain both intimate relationships and friendships. You also need to be able to search for and find common ground with people that are different than you or those that you are in disagreement with. When you are emotionally mature, your social skills and abilities include:

- having great communication skills

- managing time efficiently and effectively

- your ability to lead and manage others

- your ability to resolve conflicts and difficult situations by means of negotiation and persuasion.

All of these models are important to understanding EQ and how to be emotionally mature. We will constantly refer back to Danial Goleman's model — the mixed trait model — and his five components when we are exploring how to increase our emotional intelligence. Now that you have a basic understanding of emotional intelligence, the components of being emotionally mature, and what it looks like to have high emotional intelligence, we are going to focus on what it means to be self-aware in the next chapter.

Chapter Three: Be Aware of Yourself

"To be yourself in a world that is constantly trying to make you something else is the greatest accomplishment." - Ralph Waldo Emerson

I have devoted an entire chapter to being aware of yourself simply because this is the most important component of being emotionally mature. Without self-awareness you have no place to begin in the journey to increasing your emotional intelligence. It really is as simple as that. Every journey or path needs a first step, and being self-aware is your first step towards being the master of your emotional intelligence.

Emotional self-awareness is where you have the skill to interpret your own emotions and how they affect your actions, your decisions, and even your performance on a particular task or job. When you are emotionally self-aware you know exactly what emotion you are feeling, when you are feeling it, and why you are feeling it. This is so much more important than I could ever stress. When you can understand the rationale behind your emotions, you are able to see how your emotions are helping or hurting you in a particular situation. Here's the thing: in social situations, when you are equipped with self-awareness, you can gain insight into how other people perceive you and you can then direct your actions and choices to either fit their idea of you or to change their idea of you.

Instead of basing your self-confidence on arbitrary and immaterial matters, you can base your self-confidence on the real understanding of emotional competence because you know that you can navigate a social situation properly. You know what your strengths are, you know how the other party feels, and that puts you in a spot of advantage. You are also able to clearly establish your own values, morals, and your personal goals and purpose. It is crucial to have this quality as a leader so that you have the ability to make the tough calls, speak with authority, and implement your vision in a way that will be well received by others.

It happens often in the workplace where those around you are not adept at performing in social interactions, and so their job performance suffers as a whole. I once worked in an office where the main office leader struggled with how he spoke to people in the workplace. Many of the other office employees called our leader a bully and had little respect for his authority. While the leader was great at the specifics of his job, he had very few people skills and so his management suffered due to this. He never listened to their ideas, he never opened the floor for everyone to feel comfortable, and he often played favorites which created a toxic work environment.

This office lead did not last very long as an office lead, because soon the whole office was turned against him. No one wanted to work for him, with him, or even under him. All interactions with him were unpleasant, and finally when the risk of losing an entire office staff came to the higher ups' attention, they had to look for the common denominator. The office leader ruled his office with anger and pride every day, and he lacked the emotional self-awareness to relate to his staff and see how they perceived him. He was put at a severe disadvantage in the workforce.

When you are in a position of leadership and you use it to torment others, or you have extreme arrogance and stubbornness, then you are most likely viewed as incompetent amongst your peers. Those are not the assets of a good leader. In fact, the antiquated times that correlated a loud voice and large presence with success are gone, and so you should hang that outfit up. Better yet, throw that particular outfit away as you get ready to step into your emotionally self-aware suit.

There was a research group that took a bunch of leaders who had strengths that spanned several different trait areas in the emotional self-awareness category and did a study on them. The Korn Ferry Hay Group was in charge of this research, and their results showed that an astonishing ninety-two percent of the teams with strengths in emotional self-awareness were the teams who had the highest energy levels and the best performance statistics. The reason for this is because leaders who are able to create positive emotional environments are ones that have higher self-awareness. They do better at motivating groups of people. In stark contrast to those results, the group who had leaders that were particularly low in the self-awareness department created toxic environments seventy-eight percent of the time. That is a lot of upset teams.

There is a reason that emotion self-awareness is the foundation for all the other components — even though it is the hardest component to track and see visible progress of. Unfortunately, you cannot simply strive to be emotionally self-aware and then never think about it again. Unlike a car that you buy once and then you are set for life, your emotional self-awareness needs to be constantly tended to — like a garden. In every moment that you feel an emotion, you need to be practicing your self-awareness so that you can continue to make accurate predictions about how you are feeling and then exhibit rational responses based on those feelings. Self-awareness does become easier the more that you use the tool, and it can become almost like second nature. A good way to practice this is to make sure that you remind yourself to mentally check in on your emotions and see what they are telling you. Do this several times a day. It will help you realize whether your behavior or actions are on the right track or if you need to make a shift in order to achieve the goals you want. Remember that these goals can be long term goals, or even short term goals that exist solely for the basis of a conversation that you are partaking in during any moment. Sometimes when your emotions get overwhelming you might feel like you need to separate yourself. A stressful or sad situation can make you want to hide in bed and not come out from under the covers for a week. Unfortunately, in a professional environment you cannot exactly wig out or go and hide under your bed. You need to be able to act appropriately and manage your emotions. That is why it is important to check in with your emotions every day. Keep in mind that while you may not be free to choose the situations that you are placed in, you are always free to choose how you will react.

Let us start by analyzing the negative emotions that you most commonly experience at work. This way we can help you come up with a plan to strategize your behaviors and reactions when faced with these emotions. It only takes a brief moment of being self-aware to gather how you are truly feeling. The difference between being a good leader and a bad leader is how you handle these negative emotions. Do you work through it and make the best choice for you and your team? Or do you let the negative emotions overwhelm you and spill into how you treat your colleagues?

A 1997 study by Cynthia Fisher revealed the most common types of negative emotions that people feel when they are at work. The list includes:

- Frustration

- Dislike

- Unhappiness

- Irritation

- Aggravation

- Anger

- Disappointment

If you work in any type of professional environment, then you are bound to have experienced any one of these emotions at any given time. But there are strategies that you can use in order to help you overcome those negative emotions so that you benefit, your team benefits, and your work performance benefits. Below I have grouped some of the common behaviors together because they overlap one another in similarities.

Frustration and Irritation

Frustration is not a new emotion, and I promise you that everyone feels this at some stage in their life. Whether it is professionally or privately, frustration can easily creep in on us and before we know it, we are acting out. Normally, you would feel frustrated when you feel like you are trapped or stuck in a situation with no sign of a way out. Sometimes just the lack of forward mobility can cause frustration as well. This can be because you are not seeing eye to eye with a colleague on a project's direction, you feel like you don't know where to take your project, you are suffering with dealing with a difficult boss, and even something as simple as your day not going according to schedule.

These feelings crop up for all kinds of reasons and at the most inopportune of times; the trick, however, is to find them and nip the feelings in the bud as soon as they begin. Frustration and irritation are emotions that can get out of control very quickly and become negative feelings like anger. You don't want your emotions to escalate negatively like that, so let us take a look at some ways to manage your frustration.

- Stop and take a look around. Sometimes you really need to take time out and think about your situation. Stop the rising panic of frustration in your chest and get to the root. Ask yourself, "Why am I feeling frustrated right now?" If it helps you to write it down then do so. Just make sure you are being specific about what is irritating you. Once you have done this, take a positive look at the situation you are in. Focus on a positive, because there always is one. For example, if you have a meeting set with a colleague and they show up ten minutes late, take that extra ten minutes to prepare for the meeting and go over what you would like to talk about. Better yet, take that ten minutes and relax. Don't let it bother you.

- Finding a positive in the frustrating situation makes all the difference. Thinking positively when you start to get frustrated can honestly make all the difference that you need in your day. It may seem like a small change, but it can have big impacts on your levels of frustration. You are choosing not to let the little things or the irritating things get to you, but rather to move past them and work with what is positive. Remember, not everything that frustrates you is done to frustrate you.

- Think about what happened when you were last frustrated or irritated. Sometimes it helps to ground ourselves. Take a look at the last time you got frustrated about a situation. More than likely the situation resolved itself and it worked out alright for all parties involved. Being frustrated is not going to help you come to any solutions. It is not worth wasting time on it when you can practice letting it all go and be positive.

Nervousness and Worrying

Work can be a daunting place. Depending on what you do, your work environment, and the stress that you experience, you might find that your fear and anxiety are causing you to be nervous at work and worry about things that are beyond your control. When you worry overtly about what happens at the workplace, you risk your mental health with the negative emotions that you allow to take control. Sometimes it helps to try some of the tips below:

- Do not allow your environment to be filled with worry. This means that if you find your colleagues are surrounded in one spot and gossiping about the latest wave of layoffs or changes in company policy, then you should make a conscious effort to avoid that area. You do not need to add additional worry to your plate. I am sure it is full enough already.

- Practice deep breathing. There are apps out for this nowadays, or you can even simply time yourself with your watch. The purpose of taking in slow and deliberate deep breaths is to slow down your heart rate. When you feel your heart pounding with worry, stop and breathe in for five seconds. Then, breathe out for the other five seconds. The only thing that you should be focused on accomplishing during this time is your breathing. Do not worry about what is stressing you, the conversation behind you, or even the next project on your plate. Just take three minutes and take at least three to five deep breaths.

- Find ways to make the situation better. If you are afraid that something negative is going to happen, then you should not just sit and wait for the shoe to drop. Think of ways that you can get ahead of the problem and make it better. Turn the negative situation into a positive one.

- Keep a journal handy and write down your anxieties and fears. Writing can be therapeutic. When you write down everything that bothers you or causes you to worry, you have a list that you can work on clearing out. You need to make time to deal with each situation that is causing you anxiety.

Anger and Aggravation

I guarantee you that if you let your anger get to you and control your behavior that it will be one of the most destructive things you do for your image in the workplace. It can be a very harmful emotion to harbor when you are at work, and honestly, when it is not handled well, anger can cause you a lot more problems than it ever solved. You want to keep a lid on your anger, but in a way that is healthy and lets you express your true emotions.

- Keep your eyes peeled for any early signals that you are feeling angry. When you practice self-awareness you are able to identify when your anger or aggravation is mounting. The earlier you recognize the feeling, the sooner that you can nip it in the bud. The sooner you get ahead of this emotion, the better for everyone involved. You can choose the way that you react to every situation—this is emotional intelligence. I get that you may be angry, but that does not mean you have to act on emotion. You can choose to act appropriately.

- When anger rises, stop immediately. Sometimes it builds up fast and comes out all at once. Just stop whatever it is that you are doing and close your eyes. Start your deep breathing to try and get yourself to calm down. Remember to focus on just your breathing so that your angry ideas and words are cut off.

- Think about what you look like when you are aggravated or angry. Do you think that you like the picture of your behavior? Are your actions something to be proud of when you are angry? You don't want to convey the wrong image of yourself to those around you, so you might want to think about what you look like when you start to get upset. Seeing someone else be angry can be scary. Do you want to be scary? I am betting the answer to that is probably no.

Dislike

New policies, new colleagues, new rules, change in management, and all other changes can be an area that causes you dislike. In fact, I bet you have had to deal with someone or something that you dislike in the workplace. The important part is to remain professional, even when you feel dislike towards a person or thing.

- Maintain respect. You will not always get to work with people you like or in environments that you like, but you would still want to be respected. Sometimes you need to put your ego to the side when you find you are having a hard time liking someone. Be courteous and respectful as you interact with them. Even if they do not give you the same courteous treatment, make sure that you maintain a level of professionalism.

- Use your assertive voice. Sometimes you do need to be firm and assertive - this does not mean be rude. If the person you are interacting with is being unprofessional, then just exit the situation until you can be calm and assertive but maintain your respectfulness. You want to be the example that they look up to, not the other way around.

Unhappiness and Disappointment

Life can be tough, and the workplace does not always take it easy on us. It is no surprise that there are times when disappointment and even unhappiness can crop up in our lives and spill out into our work. These emotions are difficult to handle because they affect the way that we are productive when we work. Disappointment and unhappiness can correlate with our energy levels and our enthusiasm. When we let these emotions take effect in our work, then we are holding ourselves back from truly achieving our full potential. By being self-aware you need to:

- Accept your current mindset. If you are feeling disappointed then acknowledge it, accept it, and make a positive change. Just because you know why you are disappointed, that does not mean that you have to continue to be disappointed. You can begin to change your mindset. For example, start to make changes in your path and get excited about those new prospects.

- Adjusts any goals you have. Sometimes we fall short of a goal we intended and that causes disappointment. Just re-evaluate your goal and adjust it so that it is more attainable. These can be small or big adjustments. Life won't always go the way we plan it to. Don't let a setback destroy your outlook.

- Journal about your feelings and thoughts. It can help to write out exactly how you are feeling in your moments of unhappiness and what the root causes are. When you are able to pin down the source or sources of your unhappiness, then you can draw a roadmap towards actual happiness. You don't have to let the unhappiness define your every thought and feeling, but you can let it propel you into a plan of action.

- Keep a smile on your face. Sometimes, amongst the greatest adversities, disappointments, and unhappiness, the best thing that you can possibly do for yourself is to smile.

These are some ways that self-awareness can help you navigate your emotions while you are at work. The potential of being emotionally self-aware definitely does not stop here, and in fact the possibilities are truly endless.

Chapter Four: Regulate Yourself

"When you control your thoughts and emotions, you control everything." - Marshall Sylver

No day will pass by without you feeling some type of emotion. They are vital, necessary, and mandatory aspects of our lives. It can be as simple as enjoying the company of a loved one or getting annoyed at a fly that won't leave you alone. Every emotion you experience, whether it is positive or negative, impacts your emotional, mental, and physical health.

The other thing about emotions is that depending on how you act, you affect your image in other people's eyes. You want to make sure that your reactions match the best and appropriate response for every social situation that you find yourself in. This is important, because imagine if you are sitting in an important meeting and you inappropriately burst out in laughter. That was not the right response when you are in a business-like setting. You might want to be taken seriously and have people listen to your ideas, but you will not if your actions don't match up with the image you want. This is where regulating your emotions really comes into play. Once you have laid the foundation for recognizing your own emotions and being self-aware, then you can build on that with self-regulation.

Like with most other theories and studies that regard the psyche, there is debate within the field that studies emotions as well. Because emotions are complicated parts of our psyche to understand, there is going to be conflicting evidence and debate amongst the scientific community. With every new year, there is more learned about the human mind and our emotional regulation than ever before. Strides are being made in the emotional field, and while psychologists might not always agree with one another, they do agree that our emotions make up every interaction that we have each day.

In 2001, a model for capturing how and when emotions are created was proposed by James Gross. He created a model made up of four stages named the "modal" model. In the modal model he uses a situation to grab the attention of a person. Then he measures how they react to the situation and what emotional response stems from their reaction.

Emotional regulation can be tricky, but it can also be very simple. Sometimes, especially when you are experiencing a positive emotion, you simply need to let your emotional response continue. For example, if you are happy that something worked out, be happy and express that happiness. You do not always need to temper your reactions; it is perfectly alright to shout out in glee at the appropriate moment. Emotional regulation is all about the right reaction for the right situation. If you know that you get frustrated, annoyed, and angry easily, then you need to offset that with techniques to calm you down. Being outraged is not always the best reaction to small inconveniences in your life. Excessive negative emotions like these could result in the loss of relationships, friendships, and even your job.

When you are unable to regulate your emotions, then you are more likely to have any number of psychological disorders. For example, depression and borderline personality disorder are both disorders that share common qualities with unregulated emotions. This is why educating yourself about emotional intelligence is so important. Most people can regulate their emotions fairly well - they simply choose not to. However, if you find that you cannot regulate your emotions no matter how hard you try on your own, then it is time to seek out help (there is no shame in this).

When you are regulating your overwhelming emotions, the best techniques to try are:

- Don't suppress your emotion every time. Regulating your emotion is not always about suppressing what you are feeling in the moment. Sometimes that can be more harmful than good. There are healthy ways for you to handle and deal with negative emotions or even overwhelming emotions. For example, when you feel like you are becoming angry at a situation and you want to let out some steam, go out and take a walk. Clear your head. Kick a small rock if you have to. But work on calming yourself down before you carry on with your day or rejoin the situation that frustrates you.

- Adapt how you handle situations. You need to be able to adapt or modify the scenario that you are in. Adapt your expectations and you should be able to easily deal with disappointment and other negative emotions. It can be hard trying to manage your negative emotions in a healthy way, but there are many methods that you can use. The most important thing to remember is that your negative emotion does not have to control you or your response. You are in charge, so when you think that you are setting your expectations too high, bring your goals down and meet those first before jumping higher hurdles.

- Shift your attention elsewhere. Disappointment can be a heavy emotion to experience, and one that is not pleasant for anyone involved in the aftermath. If you are having a hard time with your expectations of yourself, set your goals lower. Sometimes we look at those in the environment around us and judge our own success off of their work. If you find yourself doing this, don't focus on the people who are succeeding the best but focus on those who are trying their best and along the same path that you are on. This helps keep you more motivated toward achieving your goals.

- Modify your thinking and your inner monologue. When you change the way that you think or what you are thinking about, then you are able to change the way that you perceive a situation. For example, if you are mad at work because you feel like someone is outshining you and that they are talking down to you as a result, shifting your mindset can make you see this scenario in an entirely different light. Instead of being the victim in this, you might change your thinking to believe that your co-worker is only trying to help your output match theirs and that they are motivating you. This does not change the situation you were in before, but it gives you an entirely new perspective on how the situation affects you. This helps you manage your own reaction and also motivates you to push yourself to do better.

- Change the way you respond. Let's say that you are unable to avoid the situation, modify your thoughts, or shift your focus away from what was bothering you. All of your emotion is now brimming on the surface and it wants to come out. You now need to use your emotional regulation in order to get yourself under control and out with the right response. For example. if your heart is racing due to a rising emotion, just breathe. Take thirty seconds to close your eyes and focus on your breathing.

Then, once you feel calmer, think about how you want to respond and carry out the correct response to the situation.

The above steps can be used to help you adapt in most social situations when your emotions are needing regulation. They mainly revolve around knowing and identifying your own emotional triggers and avoiding them. The ability to change how you are thinking and correct your behavior with rational thought is also a huge part of regulating emotions.

There is a driving force behind emotional regulation, and that is motivation. Without motivation we would not feel propelled towards our goals. According to Danial Goleman, there are four elements that comprise motivation:

- personal drive

- commitment to our goals

- initiative/readiness to take opportunities

- optimism/resilience

These elements all work together in order to help you become a more successful and motivated person when it comes to your emotional self-awareness and your self-regulation. In any career that you take part in, you are going to need more than just "smarts" to make it. In fact, you are going to need to be motivated so that the quality of work that you are delivering every time is exceptional and at your full capability.

This really comes into play when you are loving what you are doing for work. Sometimes you don't even have to love what you are doing, but you need to at least enjoy the work that you are doing. Why? Research has proven that when you enjoy your work, you are a more productive person and your output results are greater.

Intrinsic motivation is a motivation that is fueled by you from the inside with your own personal desire to overcome challenges and adversity. You desire to give high quality results at work and to be liked and trusted by your work mates.

There is also extrinsic motivation in which factors that are external are your champions. When you look at the factors of extrinsic motivation they can include (but are definitely not limited to): pay raises, bonus checks, time off, potential threat of earning no money or job loss. These are some pretty motivating factors to do your best at the job that you find yourself in.

Both intrinsic and extrinsic modes of motivation are one hundred percent okay to be fueled by; the important part is just to identify which motivation you respond to best so that you can use these methods in the future to motivate yourself when you are having a hard time. Normally, you want to be able to relax a little in the job that you work. By relax, I mean have the ability to look around and feel content because you love what you are doing. Motivation comes naturally when that is the case.

Do you think that you are motivated in life and at your job? Most studies done show that those who are motivated are able to quickly and easily adapt and more often than not they have bright attitudes when at work. Who doesn't love working with happy souls all day? Much better than working with grumpy ones! Most employers want motivated individuals because this means that their own reputation gets boosted by having a positive employee. There are also a lot less call outs when people enjoy coming in to work. Both methods of motivation are fine, however being intrinsically motivated reaps rewards personally and professionally a lot faster. This is why you see so many jobs trying to focus on promoting a healthy work culture.

Take a moment and think about those people in your life. I am sure there is at least one person that you look at in awe because no matter what the social situation is, tense, awkward, funny, etc., they always handle it well and appropriately. This is merely emotional intelligence on display, and you can manage to boost your own, too.

I don't need to beat a dead horse by repeating to you what emotional intelligence is, but I do want to add that there is no debate amongst the experts about how important it is. There is a general consensus that your EQ plays a major role in your success in all areas of your life. Gone are the days when IQ was the sole driving force of the smart, but now without EQ you do not fall into those same categories of intelligence. This is because your EQ drives not just your intellectual performance but also all other emotion based decisions that you make.

Every day we are led by our emotions, whether that is in joyful situations or even painful situations. When we feel excited at new opportunities we take chances to make them work, when we are hurt we will cry, and when we love we sacrifice for what we love. If you try and state that your emotions play no part in any decision that you make then you are not giving them enough credit and you are definitely hindering your ability to truly become in touch with your emotions. There is nothing to be gained from acting like the "macho man."

Navigating your emotions is a delicate balancing act at the end of each day. This is because you want to make sure that you are balanced and not lacking or in excess of any particular emotion. This is why being able to express your emotions in a positive and healthy manner is prize one, because you are able to control your emotional response to external stimuli.

Our negative emotions are particularly susceptible to occurring in excess or being hard to control and navigate. This is especially true in the heat of the moment when a person might be feeling overwhelmed by their emotional response. If negative emotions such as rage, bitterness, and even envy are allowed to take root and fester within a person's mind, then there are some detrimental effects that can affect the quality of life that you have. This can look like someone who is always angry, or a person who is constantly sad. These aren't ways that we are born, but consequences of emotions that were allowed to build until that is all that was left. We want to feel our negative emotions, but in a healthy and positive way, not in a way that is allowed to fester within our minds. There are six steps that can be practiced in order to make sure that you control your emotional response, make sure your decisions are made with rational reasoning, and manage emotionally challenging situations:

- Never react at first. When you first feel an emotional response rise up you need to recognize it before merely acting on impulse. This is particularly true with negative emotions, because you do not want to say or do something which will bring you regret or shame later. Take a breath, steady yourself, and think about your response and make sure that it is rational. Don't answer when your heart is racing or you are in fight or flight mode.

- Rely on and ask for guidance. You can ask for guidance from those around you or even seek guidance within a faith. It does not matter what faith you decide to rely on, as long as you are able to ask for help and wisdom in combating the obstacles that stand in your emotional intelligence journey.

- Look for or create a healthy way to express yourself. When you have learned how to control your emotions, you need to also find ways to let out any emotions you are feeling in a healthy way. You do not want to repress your emotions, bottle them up, or avoid them until they get so big that they explode. This can take form in many different ways. For some, they just need a trusted person to vent to, and a call or a text can often be the perfect solution. Others find hobbies like painting, writing, or even running to express the negative emotions that they are feeling. Meditation, physical activity, journaling, etc. are all just healthy ways of expressing your emotions and letting them out. As long as it is helping you, do it.

- Take a look at the bigger picture. Sometimes we focus so much on the here and now that we forget there is a bigger picture to look at and live by. Everything that we do serves a purpose towards an ultimate goal. Simply because you don't understand why something is happening in the moment does not mean that it does not have a purpose. Understand and trust that there are factors outside of your control and that there is always a bigger purpose in this life.

- Change your thinking. When you experience constant negative thoughts, then you are allowing yourself to enter a negative cycle. When you feel like an emotion is cropping up that is leaving you disheartened or is draining you because of its negative pattern, then you need to work to change it. Engage in an activity or even merely focus on the positives in your life to drive out the negative thought processes. Replace these negative thoughts with happier thoughts.

- Be forgiving to yourself for your triggers. Sometimes triggers are great - when we get happy or excited in the moment and express that towards our loved ones. And other times, triggers are not so great - when we feel angry and we become outwardly upset or frustrated. You want to be able to make sure that your emotional triggers work, but that you temper them with rational thought before responding. At the same time, forgive yourself. Don't be hard on yourself when you feel irritated because the same commercial played on television five times in a row. Allow the irritation to pass, then forgive yourself. Don't dwell on it and do not beat yourself up about it. Forgiving yourself allows you to detach yourself from the negative emotions.

I cannot stress enough how much humans rely on emotions for their everyday interactions and functions. We are emotional beings - and that one hundred percent includes us men. There will forever be moments where emotions crop up, we feel certain things, and we want to react in ways out of impulse. Take a time out when you feel your emotions becoming overwhelming. You will thank yourself when you do. Sometimes, all you need is a moment of clarity to master your emotions.

Chapter Five: Recognizing Emotions

"Emotions are the most powerful things to recognize and honor. Don't discourage your feelings." - Bindu Lamba

Most people have trouble identifying their own emotions, much less the emotions that those around them are feeling. However, it is an important skill and when it comes to emotional intelligence, it is a skill that you cannot move forward without. This is worth investing time into so that you can learn how to perceive your own emotions and also the emotions of those around you.

If you seem to have trouble right now recognizing or identifying what you are feeling at any given point, take a look at some of the tips below and apply them to your own life. Maybe take a moment now to analyze how you are feeling by using this list!

Firstly, look at your physical response. The first place your emotions are most likely to manifest is within your body, and you can tell by your body's impulse reaction to your emotion. For example, you want to look out for:

- Pain or tightness in the stomach: could indicate sadness, distrust, betrayal

- Blush spreading across face and neck: could indicate happiness or even embarrassment

- Tightness in the chest or tensing of muscles: could indicate fear or anxiety

Your physical reactions might very well be different to the ones described above, and that is okay. Your job is to become familiar with what your physical responses are. When you feel yourself having a physical response to an emotion, simply stop and ask yourself why you would be acting that way.

Secondly, you need to try and identify what you are feeling. I know this might sound easier said than done, but you want to put the work in here. If you need to, draw or download a chart of feelings or even a wheel (if you want to make it a fun game) and use this to pinpoint and identify what emotion relates to the feelings and thoughts that you are having at a particular moment.

Thirdly, you need to avoid judging yourself or your emotions. Embrace the emotions that you experience. They are a part of you. Not a part that needs to be hidden away, or a part that you need to be embarrassed about. Everyone feels. As a man I know it can be hard to express those feelings because we have been taught that it somehow makes us less than other men, but it does not. When you confront and accept your feelings head on then you are less likely to have emotional outbursts from repressing or judging them.

My fourth point to you is that sometimes you just need to stay still. It can be easy to move quickly and cycle through emotions just as fast as our movements, especially when we want to get over the negative emotions we are experiencing. However, sometimes you need to sit with your emotions, see how you are feeling, and address them. Meditation helps with this, but if you just want to go ahead and spend ten minutes in peace where you are not fighting your emotions then that works, too.

Writing is an amazing outlet, and that brings us to our fifth area to work on when trying to recognize our emotions. There

74

are therapeutic qualities to writing, and when you are able to get your thoughts, ideas, and emotions onto paper, that is a whole lot less left to jumble around in your mind. Try writing a stream of consciousness (this is where you do not stop to think about what you are writing, you just write, write, write continuously for ten or fifteen minutes).

When you are overwhelmed or trying to process emotion, you should lean into someone. Talking to someone is my sixth tip for you, and one that you should not undervalue. This does not have to be in the form of a therapist, and sometimes meeting with a friend for coffee and explaining how you are feeling can give you some clarity. There is nothing bad about showing vulnerability to your loved ones. In fact, only good can come from that.

On another note, music has been an excellent escape for many. Whether you play music or you listen to music you can find a way to let out exactly what you are feeling. There are millions of songs out there that are devised to help us pour our emotions out. You might just try finding a quiet spot and listening to some music that suits your mood.

Finally, you should take some time before you go to sleep every single day and you should reflect on what happened during your day. This daily reflection can help you sort through the different emotions that you encountered as you lived your day. Sometimes you can record this in a journal, or if you prefer to internalize it in a monologue that is okay, too. As long as you are sorting through the emotions you felt, then you are actively working to identify and recognize your own emotions and how they affect you.

"Let's not forget that the little emotions are the great captains of our lives and we obey them without realizing it." – Vincent Van Gogh

Those are some wise words by Vincent Van Gogh, but accurate words as well. Our smallest feelings can impact us in great ways and we should always pay attention to all our feelings; even if we are tempted to ignore them as inconsequential emotions.

Learning how to recognize these emotions is the first step to helping us regulate and manage our emotions. Ignoring your emotions will only create a build up or pent up and unexpressed emotion, which can cause a scene when it all comes crashing out of you all at once. Make sure that you give yourself time to analyze and interpret your emotions before you move past them and onto the next thing. When you finally are able to interpret your emotions, that is the beginning of your healthy decisions. You do need to be honest with yourself, and this can be a scary thought at times. Take comfort in knowing that you are not the only man out there with feelings and that your honesty will only take you further along your journey to mastering your emotional intelligence.

Recognizing Emotions

Marsha Linehan, who is the doctor that created a therapy known as Dialectical Behavior Therapy (DBT), has created a process that involves six steps towards recognizing your own emotions. You need to put in the work, but the process goes as follows:

1 - What happened?

During this step you write down or describe in full detail the emotional issue that is plaguing you. Don't get caught up in the he said/she said and write down just the facts of the event.

2 - Why do you think that this event happened?

In this part, you want to identify the reasoning you believed caused the emotional situation to arise. It is important to think about the why because this will allow you to easily identify what social interaction garnered a response from you and then how you could best approach that interaction in the future. Correcting your negative emotional behavior with rational thought is super helpful in your future interactions and can prevent emotional events from happening in the future.

3 - How did this event make you feel both emotionally and physically?

Now you want to make sure that you record both your first emotional responses and your secondary emotional responses to the situation. Also, note down how your body physically reacted to your emotions. Did your jaw tighten? Did you clench your fists? Did you pout or cry? All of these are important in understanding and defining your emotional outputs.

4 - What did you want to do because of your emotions?

When you think about this question, be honest with your answer. You need to think about and identify your emotional urges to your feelings. Sometimes it is hard or it can even hurt when we admit the actions we want to take when we were in the heat of the moment. But it is important to take stock of what you wanted to say or do so that you can be aware of your emotional response and know how and where to rationalize your behavior in the future. Simply because it was an urge that you had, that does not mean you have to act upon it. There are ways to control your urges when you are in the middle of an emotional battle.

5 - What did you do and say?

You need to identify how your emotions led you into certain behavior. Even if the behavior you displayed was less than favorable, you still need to be honest about the way that you handled the event so that you can make corrective behavior changes in the future.

6 - How did your emotions and actions later affect you?

Finally, you need to list what the long term ramifications for your actions were. Did your words or reactions leave an effect on your life or someone else's life? Did you handle your emotions well or do you have regrets about what you said or did? You want to hold yourself responsible for the way that you act, what you do, and what you say. We are free to make our own choices and conduct our own behaviors, but we are not free from those consequences.

As you find yourself in another emotional event, take a moment to really rationalize your behavior. Use this list to analyze what the real problem is, what the root of your emotions are, and then how to proceed forward in the best possible manner.

Body Language

I have spoken a lot about body language in passing, and now I want to really focus more in depth on it, because when you are trying to understand and recognize the emotions of others, body language is going to be your best friend.

Body language includes the non-verbal signals that we use when we communicate. Most of our communication is actually non-verbal through every single interaction that we have. This can be from facial expressions, body movements, the space our body takes up, and even lack of body movement. All of the things that we do with our body communicates how we are feeling. In fact, your daily communication is about seventy percent body language! That is a huge chunk of communication that is not coming from your words. This is why you want to focus on two things: What your body language is telling others, and what others are telling you with their body language.

Facial Expressions

A picture tells a thousand words, and that is mainly because we interpret body language when looking at pictures. Our facial expressions can give away a lot of what we are thinking and feeling. A simple smile can convey happiness, while a frown can signal unhappiness. A raised eyebrow might show interest or surprise and an open mouth could indicate shock. Even if you tell someone that you are fine, they can often scan your face and see how you really are faring. In fact, a few of the emotions that can be read from facial expressions are:

- Happiness

- Fear

- Anger

- Sadness

- Excitement

- Surprise

- Desire

- Disgust

- Confusion

- Contempt

When we are analyzing a person's facial expressions we make split second decisions on whether to believe what they are telling us or whether they are lying. When it comes to universal language, facial expressions make it into the top ten because many of the basic expressions such as anger, sadness, and happiness are expressed through the same facial patterns throughout the world.

Facial expressions are so important in our interactions with other people. In fact, studies have shown that we make judgements about the intelligence of other people based solely on their facial expressions and the look of their faces. Someone with a more prominent nose accompanied by a narrow face was perceived as an intelligent person. Likewise, those who had a smile and expressed joy with their facial expressions were believed to be more intelligent than those who demonstrated angry expressions. Below, I am going to outline several areas of the face and how they are used for expression and communication.

Your Eyes

I am sure you have heard the eyes called "windows to the soul." This is because they are able to show others a lot about what you are thinking or feeling. When you talk to someone else and you stay engaged with the conversation, focus on their eye movements. They say that maintaining eye contact is an important part of communication and here's why:

When someone is avoiding your gaze, blinking too much or their pupils dilate, then you are getting a lot of information about their emotional state. Each eye signal tells you what the person might be feeling, and that allows you to react in a way that might best fit the outcome for the conversation that you are looking for.

Eye gaze is important. If a person is maintaining eye contact with you and looking in your eyes, it means that they take an interest in what you are saying. You know that they are paying attention to you. However, this can take a turn when the eye contact becomes prolonged, as it can appear threatening when coupled with a dark glare. If a person constantly breaks your eye contact or looks away from you a lot, it might mean that they are uncomfortable in the conversation, distracted, and even possible trying to hide their true emotions in the moment.

Blinking is a natural part of providing your eyes with lubrication. However, sometimes you can tell if a person blinks way too fast or way too slow. In a distressed situation or a situation where the other party is uncomfortable, they may appear to blink a lot faster. If they blink slowly or infrequently then that is a sign that the person is intentionally trying to control what their eyes are telling you by controlling all movements.

The size of a person's pupils is the most subtle non-verbal form of communication that comes from the eyes. Light levels can impact pupil size, but so can emotions. For example, if you are talking to someone and their pupils become highly dilated, then they are most likely interested in you or aroused by your presence/what you are saying.

Your Mouth

Your mouth tells a lot about what you are thinking and feeling, even when you do not want it to. It can be as subtle as chewing on your lip in public subconsciously, but that automatically conveys to others that you are experiencing either anxiety or worrying about something. Sometimes in public people will cover their mouths in conversations. This is a polite effort if you are going to yawn or cough, however it can also be used to hide a frown or disapproving twist of the mouth. Even your smile can be read in more than one way, and it does not always express feelings of happiness. A smile can be sarcastic, happy, and even sinister in nature.

Pursed lips appear in the tightening of a person's mouth. This shows distaste and disapproval, and at times it can also be an indicator that the person thinks you are acting or being distasteful.

When you bite your lip it can indicate that you are worried, stressed, and even anxious about something.

Covering the mouth is mainly used in conversation when people are trying to mask their true emotional reactions. For example, if they smirk at something you said but don't want to offend you then they might cover their mouth.

If your mouth is turned up or down it can indicate a lot about how you are feeling. Slight changes in the mouth's curves can mean a lot. For example a curve upward normally indicates happiness and optimism, while a turn down of the mouth's curves can show sadness, disapproval, or even a grimace of disgust or anger.

Your Gestures

Gestures are direct signs of body language that are easy to interpret and are almost always going on when in conversation with someone. There is a large amount of movement that is classified under gestures but they do include waving, pointing, and even simply using your hands to articulate a point.

Gestures can be some of the most direct and obvious body language signals. It is important to note that not all gestures are the same culturally and they do vary by culture, so make sure that you are familiar with the gestures of the culture you are interacting with. Here are some of the more common gestures:

A closed or clenched fist illustrates anger, but depending on the context it can also mean that you stand in solidarity with others.

When you give a thumbs up or down to someone you are normally communicating that you either approve or disapprove of something.

When you touch your thumb and your index finger together to form a circle gestures that everything is "okay." This is mainly in mainstream American culture and I would be careful using it in other cultures as it might not imply the same connotation of being all right.

In many countries when you hold up your index and middle finger to make a V shape it is indicative that you are throwing up a peace sign. Again, this is not how it is seen in all countries, so unless you are familiar with the gestures of that country you should refrain from making this sign.

Your Arms and Legs

Your arms and legs say a lot that your words might not be saying. You can cross your arms in a defensive manner, or you can even move your legs away from someone in a signal that you are not comfortable with that person. There are a lot of subtle ways that our bodies communicate even when we are not speaking or engaged in conversation. For example, take a look at what you might be saying with your arms and legs:

Crossing your arms signals that you are feeling defensive or that you are closed-off and not receptive to advances. It can also mean that you are protecting yourself.

If you place your hands on your hips it might show that you are in control of what is going on. Alternatively, it is also a sign that you are upset or aggressive.

You might clasp your hands together behind your back every now and then, but it normally indicates that you are either bored or anxious about something.

An impatient, frustrated, and even bored person might tap their fingers on a desk or object, and even fidget a lot to show how they are feeling.

When you cross your legs you are also indicating that you are closed off. It can also signify that you want to be left alone or given privacy.

Posture

Posture is an important part of how we hold our bodies in relation to the space around us. It is also an indicator for others to read our body language. When you are observing someone, their posture can tell you a lot about what they are feeling; but it doesn't end there, because posture can also relay a lot of information about their personalities. If you're trying to figure out whether someone is receptive to you, confident in their abilities, submissive to those around them, and even closed off to advances, you can look at their posture and make an informed decision based on their body language.

For example, when someone sits up straight, this shows that they are being attentive to the area around them or a particular scene. Now, if that same person is sitting up but hunched over their posture is telling us that they are bored with the scene in front of them.

As you are practicing your skills at reading body language, pay attention to what a person's posture is indicating to you:

- Open posture is where their upper body will be exposed. That means they won't have their hands cross across their chest or stomach. When a person has posture that is open, that means they are open to friendly advances, and willing to listen to or go along with suggestions.

- Closed posture is where you see that the person is closing or hiding their upper body. They can either hunch over or cross their arms around their body or cross their legs. When a person exhibits a closed posture this means that they aren't open to advances, they could have anxiety, and it could even be a display of hostility.

Your Personal Space

If you have never said that you just need your personal space, then I am sure that you have at least heard someone tell you they need personal space. If you have felt a need for personal space, you might become uncomfortable when a person stands too close to you or hovers over you.

Edward T. Hall, an anthropologist, created four different levels of social distance when he created the idea of proxemics. Proxemics is merely the distance that exists between people who are interacting.

Intimate Distance is a space of 6-18 inches. When you are this close to one another it normally signals that you have a close relationship with the person you are interacting with and there is a comfort that exists in the space between you.

Personal Distance is a space of 1.5-4 feet. This level of physical distance occurs normally between family members and close friends. You can tell the level of intimacy in a relationship by whether they maintain personal or intimate distance.

Social distance is a space of 4-12 feet. Normally this level of distance happens between people who are acquaintances. Meaning that you know them, but you are not familiar enough with them to feel comfortable standing or interacting in a space closer than this.

Public distance is a space of 12-25 feet. At this level, you are normally in a public setting with people you don't know. You might be giving a public presentation or teaching a class.

While the level of space a person wants and feels comfortable at can vary depending on their culture, you should still try and respect the personal space that a person creates between you and them. When you have a stronger grasp on body language and what it is telling you, you will pick up on these subtle social cues a lot faster. It will also make your interactions a lot more pleasant.

Remember that you don't want to analyze every minute body language or facial expression on its own, but as a whole together. Often a smile on its own does not tell us as much as the posture of the shoulders, body placement, eye expression, and eyebrow raise might tell us when combined with that smile.

Chapter Six: Social Skills

"Communication - the human connection - is the key to personal and career success" - Paul Meyer

Empathy is simply a person's ability to recognize and share the emotions that someone else is experiencing. This could be a real person or even a fictional person. When a person is truly empathetic they can see a situation from the other party's perspective as well as share the emotions and distress that person is feeling.

Sometimes people can confuse demonstrating empathy with having pity, sympathy, or even compassion. While these are similar to one another, they focus more on the plight of others while empathy focuses on a shared experience. For example, pity is when you feel uncomfortable over someone else's behavior or feelings and you use a condescending or paternalistic tone to convey your pity. When pity is dealt out, it is being said that the object of the pity does not deserve what is happening to them and that they are unable to change their own fortune around. When you pity someone you do not engage with them on the same level that you would when you empathize with them.

When you display sympathy you are showing that you care and have concern for someone that is close to you. Normally, when you sympathize with someone you want to see them happier, or even just doing better than they are doing currently. Sympathy does connect more on a shared level of experience with the other person, but it does not involve you sharing their perspective or their emotions.

Compassion is considered akin to being right alongside

another person. It is more engaged with the individual than empathy is, and normally the goal of feeling compassionate is to alleviate the stress of the other person. Empathy is where you can share a person's emotions, but compassion goes a step further and builds on empathy.

Sometimes even when you have empathy, it can be hard to know what to do or what to say in a social situation. You feel with the person that you are talking to, but you have a hard time finding the right words because it seems like nothing you say can affect the moment. This happens all the time. Simply because you can empathize does not mean that you magically know all the right things to say and do. This is why empathy is made up of a component of skills that you can use to your benefit to help you navigate sticky social situations. We will cover ways to offer help, control your own emotions, take action, learn when not to act, and following up with the person.

Responding With Empathy

1 - Offer your help. Not everyone that you come across will need or want your help. Sometimes they do want help, but your help is not the help that they are after. This can be hard for some people to get over, but the truth is that when you are empathizing you need to respect their wishes. Practicing empathy is not about your innate need to feel better or help, but rather the person that you are connecting with. Talk to them and find out what the best way to help would be. They might want your advice, a shoulder to cry on, help to and from work, and they might not even want your help. When you see someone in need and you feel their need, offer to help and then respect their decision to accept or reject that help.

2 - Control your emotions. Emotion contagion is how you are

able to feel the emotion that another person is experiencing. Feeling what the other person feels is a necessary part of empathy, but if you let it overwhelm you then you might not be able to help the person you are empathizing with.

3 - Take action. If a person wants your help, then get into gear and get moving. It can be hard to know whether you are taking the right action or not, but your empathy will help drive you toward the right decision. A good way to help if they do not indicate a specific way that they need help would be to ask yourself what you would want done if you were in their shoes.

4 - Know when to withhold action. Not everyone will want your help. In fact, some people just want to be left to their own devices in their own space. They could want that for a variety of reasons that include simply needing their time to sort out their emotions. It might be that they don't feel completely comfortable with you just yet. It is just as important to know when not to do anything as it is to know when to do something. Even if you want to help with every fiber of your being, you still need to remove your own wishes and respect the wishes of the person that is in need.

5 - Follow up. You might have helped the person, or you might have done nothing per their wishes. The important part is that no matter what you chose to do, you follow up. You don't just walk away and fail to follow through. When you leave people alone when you feel like they are no longer in a tough spot, they might find themselves isolated and alone. It is always a good idea just to check in on them and let them know that you are there.

The other thing you should keep in mind is that suffering does not go away overnight. If you knew that someone had an issue, don't assume it went away just because they no longer talk about it. Reach out to them and check in on them - you don't have to talk about their problem necessarily. Make sure that you keep the lines of communication open to them. These techniques are devised to help you maneuver a situation in which you need to practice your empathy. Contrary to the world's popular belief, not every problem needs a solution. Sometimes all a person needs is someone who understands why they feel the way they do.

Dealing with Negative Emotions

Positive and negative emotions are both a standard part of life. Without one we cannot have the other. Sometimes, though, we struggle to appropriately express our negative emotions and they can build up and cause some serious issues and harm to our health if we do not know how to handle them. While it is an easy fix to lash out when you are feeling sad, angry, and even fearful, this won't help you deal with your real emotions or the event that brought up the emotions. Emotions that do not get dealt with can end up being managed in harmful ways such as:

Denial: A person will refuse to accept that something is wrong or that they need help. People often deny that they have any negative emotions or feelings that are causing problems. These bottled up and pent up feelings end up exploding at some point and can cause harm to the person in denial and those within firing range.

Withdrawal: a person might not want to be around anyone or hang out and participate in activities that they once liked. There is a pivotal difference between wanting your solitude every now and then and withdrawing yourself from social interaction consistently. Withdrawal is one of the first signs of depression, and can also be an indication that the person is ashamed about something that they have done or are feeling.

Bullying: a person that threatens, forces others to do their will, and ridicules in order to possess power is bullying those around them. When a person bullies another it is indicative that they have shortcomings (or perceived shortcomings) in their own selves and so they lash out at others. The object of bullying is to feel better about oneself by putting down those around them.

Self-harm: is a serious and dangerous result of unregulated negative emotions. This can take the form of cutting, starving, binge eating and purging, and any other behavior that leads to physical, mental, or even emotional harm. Those who self-harm often feel like it is a reprieve from the emotional distress that they are in.

Substance use: when a person uses alcohol or drugs in an inappropriate manner in order to feel numb to the world and their emotions, they are participating in substance abuse. This form of abuse can have serious effects on their brain, causing damage and in cases of over use of alcohol and drugs it can even cause death. When using substances that are addictive and mind numbing, it can increase the likelihood that the person will have suicidal thoughts or create a lifelong addiction. If this is ever a concern for you or someone that you know, find ways to get help. Speak to someone. Involve other people that are going to be objective.

This is why I stress the importance of being able to regulate and express all of your emotions, even the negative ones. I want you to have healthy and balanced emotional health. A good way to deal with your negative emotions can be to practice PATH:

- Pause

- Acknowledge

- Think

- Help

Pause: this is step one and it involves you stopping instead of immediately reacting to your feelings. When you stop and think about things you gain a new perspective. So take a deep breath and count to 100 if you need to. The point is that you need to truly pause.

Acknowledge: step two is where you acknowledge whatever emotion you are feeling and know that it is completely okay to feel that way. You can feel however you want and are entitled to that.

Think: by step three you have now thought about your emotions and acknowledged that you have a right to feel them. But in step three you need to think about what the right response is to the situation that you are in. This means thinking about what you are feeling and what will make the feeling better.

Help: step four is your time to take action and put into motion the plan that you came up with in step three.

Different Ways to Help Yourself Express Emotions

Sometimes we need a little help figuring out constructive ways to express our emotions. So, I want to give you a list to work with. This can help you become more comfortable expressing your full range of emotions if you are not there just yet.

Boost your Mood:

- Read a story of a person that you admire

- Play with an animal

- Clean up your space or reorganize your space

- Create a travel list

- Watch a program that offers comedic relief

Cater to your Basic Needs

- Drink some water

- Take a hot shower or even a relaxing bath

- Take a nap if you need one

- Eat a healthy meal or snack

Process your Feelings

- Punch a punching bag (a pillow works too)

- Scream to let out frustration

- Cry if you need to (because it's completely okay to do so)

- Rip up paper

- Draw or write about how you are feeling

- Write out a list of things you are grateful for

Never underestimate the power of a good venting session. This is not where you are asking for help, but rather where you use someone as a sounding board for your feelings. Sometimes all you need is to say how you are feeling out loud without being judged. Sometimes writing a letter that you never send helps you vent without needing to talk to anyone. I advise you to partake in whatever methods help you vent safely. My only caution is to avoid social media, as people can misconstrue your venting and this can lead to more negative feelings.

If you feel overwhelmed by your problems, write every single problem down in a list. Then, with the help of a friend or even family, find solutions to some of those problems, and take it one small step at a time.

You are a person of strength as well. When we experience negative emotions we can forget that fact. Write down what your strengths are on a list and appreciate that sometimes you simply are just amazing.

Practice Acts of Kindness

- Help out a stranger

- Volunteer at a cause you care about

- Do something selfless for a friend or family

Stress Relievers and Hobbies

- Play a game that you love

- Start a garden, get the material and learn to plant something new

- Write a story, or express your feelings on paper

- Create a craft project that allows you to immerse yourself

There are a myriad of ways that you can help yourself or things that can fit your needs in order to express your emotions in a truly healthy way. You might find that none of these techniques are helping you.

I strongly advise that if you find yourself recurrently struggling with expressing your negative emotions in a healthy way that you seek out professional help. You don't want to suffer silently with anxiety or depression.

There are online websites such as mhascreening.org that you can go to for help in regards to taking free screening tests or even looking for resources for your next steps or where to seek help. My only goal is that you find a way to get in touch with your emotions and that you find healthy ways to express them.

Yes, you are a man. And men feel, too.

Chapter Seven: 30 Day Emotional Intelligence Booster Program

This is probably the most important part of this guide that you have been waiting for - a thirty day guide to boosting your emotional intelligence. Don't get me wrong, the first half of this book provides you with invaluable information about understanding emotional intelligence, the components of emotional intelligence, and what you can do in order to help yourself be more self-aware, self-regulated, motivated, empathetic, and socially aware. However, now we are going to practice everything that you learned and you will have thirty days to boost your EQ.

I will be with you through every step in this journey. Don't worry, it is going to be practical, easy to follow and understand, and I will have a wealth of resources and examples for you to lean on as you battle your way into a higher state of emotional intelligence over the next month. You will need to keep yourself motivated and on task, though. It is helpful if you get a journal that you can write within each day and tackle your emotions and problems so that you can continue to progress. Every single day for the next thirty days needs to be started and finished with you being consciously aware of your emotions.

At the end of every day you need to set aside time and analyze what happened in your day, how you responded to each situation, and if that was the appropriate response. It is important to write down and evaluate your day every day over these next thirty days in order for the program to work. Trust me, you will be excited to come in at the end of the day and see how you did and how you are improving in your EQ skills.

Days 1-5: Getting to Know Yourself

Day One

"Knowing yourself is the beginning of all wisdom." - Aristotle

Today is day one of your journey into boosting your EQ. I am going to start by saying congratulations on starting! This is a big step as a man to decide to break societal conventions and for the sake of your emotional health take learning into your own hands. Every day for the next five days we are going to practice getting to know yourself better. This is the first step towards self-awareness. If you want to brush up some more on the reasons why self-awareness is so important, go back to Daniel Goleman's model of the mixed model in chapter two and give yourself a refresher. This journey is going to be broken into his five main components so that you can focus on yourself, then others as you learn to navigate the emotional minefield.

In a separate journal I want you to document each day what happened, how things happened, and your response. However, we are going to take it one step further than this.

On the first day of your journal I want you to write down your goal. For the first five days we are going to aim to recognize when we are feeling the basic six emotions that we went over in chapter one:

- anger

- disgust

- happiness

- sadness

- surprise

- fear

Once you recognize when you are feeling each emotion, your goal is to identify the emotion and your choices that stem from it. For day one, however, we will simply focus on recognizing emotions.

At the beginning of today, write down how you currently identify and label emotions or feelings that you go through in your day. I also want you to write down each of the six basic emotions and how you think you would typically feel when you are experiencing these emotions. For example, you can write down: "When I feel sad, my body seems to slow down and I don't seem to function quite as quickly as is normal for me. My body feels weighed down by sadness." You don't have to go in depth with the answer unless you want to. You can keep it short and sweet.

Then, go live your day. Go about your day as you would normally. If you can pay extra attention to your emotions and what you are feeling in an attempt to identify them then great! If not, that's okay. The point of today is to get you comfortable with your emotions and to start you on your goals.

At the end of the day, take some time on your own and get your journal out. On this page of your journal I want you to write out every emotion that you can recall feeling today. Leave some space by each emotion because we are going to go back in and fill in some information about the feeling you felt.

Now that you have established the emotions you recognized, go back and write down what you believe triggered every emotion.

For example, if you wrote down that you felt happy you also need to write down what event or person made you feel that way. And how did you react as a result of this emotion? Do you think that you reacted in the appropriate manner for the emotion?

If you felt a positive emotion, I want you to write down if it helped solve any problems or situations that you faced. Vice versa, if you felt a negative emotion I want you to write down how that emotion influenced the situation you were in. Then reflect on each emotion and congratulate yourself again. You managed to go through your first day of navigating emotions. If you are feeling discouraged by the end of day one, give yourself a break. Understand that this is a thirty day process and it will take time before you show progress in boosting your EQ.

Day Two - Four

"Honesty and transparency make you vulnerable. Be honest and transparent anyway." - Mother Teresa

Days two, three, and four will follow the same patterns and exercises as one another. The reason is because the goal of these days is to get you comfortable with recognizing emotions. You should see your abilities at feeling and recognizing your emotions improve with each day that passes. On these days I want you to remember the words from the quote above. There is nothing wrong with vulnerability, despite what the world tells you as a man. You need to be honest with yourself for this process to work. You need to stop masking your emotions under anger and pride. Do not be afraid to truly feel your emotions.

Your Exercise:

For each of the next three days you are going to pause throughout your day. If you can manage to pause every hour from when you wake up to when you get home that is the most ideal. Set a timer on your phone if you have to remind yourself to pause. Then, with each pause, focus on identifying the emotion that you are currently experiencing. Write the emotion down in your journal or someplace that you can later transfer to your journal when you get ready to do your journaling. It is possible to feel more than one emotion at a time. If you find yourself in this situation, simply write down every single emotion that you are feeling.

This exercise is extremely important to your success. It might seem repetitive, but it is helping you learn to use muscles that you are not accustomed to using. Your mental muscles are getting exercise when you name each emotion while you feel them through your body. When you name the emotions and write them down, then you are forcing yourself to physically think about your emotions as well, not just simply react to how you are feeling without thought.

I want to stress a point about your emotions. While men do use anger and pride as a mask for their other emotions, that does not mean that these are not healthy or valid emotions to experience. You are perfectly valid if you do feel angry, however you need to be able to control your response and express this anger in a healthy and mature way. Emotions like anger can be turned into a positive emotion and do not always have to be a negative emotion. Remember, every emotion we feel is an emotion that has been developed for a reason.

Day Five

"Learn to know yourself... to search realistically and regularly the processes of your own mind and feelings." - *Nelson Mandela*

On day five, I want you to keep your exercise in mind and still work on that today. Don't drop the ball now that you are getting the hang of it. You should still be journaling at least once a day, but preferably twice a day. The optimal way to journal would be to wake up in the morning, write down what your goals for the day are, then at the end of the day I want you to record the emotions that you felt, the way you handled the emotions, and how you reacted to the situations you were placed in. You need to always keep in mind that while you cannot control your impulse emotion, you can always control how you react and what you do after you feel the emotion arise.

Day five is really where you should be comfortable with identifying your emotions — even if it is just privately for right now. There is no requirement that you have to be open with everyone yet. It is a big step just to admit to yourself that yes, you do feel something other than anger and pride.

You can record all sorts of interactions that you have and how you handled them. I did this program myself as I was testing it out before implementing it in this guide, so I am going to share an excerpt of my own journal at each step. This is what my journal looked like on day five:

"Today's goals are:

- recognize and notate what emotions I feel every few hours and in situations that stir up emotion

- regulate my responses as best I can for my emotions

- be honest with myself about the emotions that I am feeling

The emotions I felt today were:

- Anger - I was running late for work because I snoozed my alarm once and then the second time I accidentally turned it off instead of snoozing it. This made me feel aggravated. I could feel my frustration stir up inside every muscle in my body and so before I walked out of the door of the house I stopped, breathed, and I felt a little better.

- happiness - I was happy for the most part. It was Friday today which means I have the whole weekend to look forward to as relaxation away from work. I felt like I was productive at work as well since I finished a big project.

- Sadness - I had been looking forward to some leftovers but they had gone off by the time I had come home. I felt sad and was able to cheer myself up by whipping up an equally delicious meal for dinner.

Interactions that I had:

- My wife and I spoke about the kids' school schedules this morning and how best to navigate our different schedules with their extra-curricular activities. I was feeling frustrated because I was running late by this point, and it spilled into the conversation, but I apologized, took a moment, and we were back on track in a healthy conversation.

- At work I had a colleague critique some of my research

and I felt hurt. I wanted to shut down but I asked about their opinions, forced myself to be objective about their input, and then gave my research a second glance. They were right about a few things and I took the opportunity to thank them and expand my research which benefited my team in the long run."

Now, your journal might look completely different from my entry, but its main goal is to track your progress. Be honest about your successes as well as your failures. There is always a chance to improve on what you did the day before, so do not beat yourself up about not being where you want to be just yet. Focus on your goals and be diligent with your journaling so you can track your progress.

Days 6-15: Improving Yourself

Day Six

"Change is your friend not your foe, change is a brilliant opportunity to grow." - Simon T. Bailey

We keep the ball rolling on day six and we take it one step further. We are going to go one step further than being self-aware; we are now going to focus on self-regulation and improving our actions. If this sounds like a lot, it is because it can be.

Self-regulation is not without its challenges, but I promise you that your improvements will be the best thing you could do for yourself. Change truly is an opportunity that you need to learn to embrace. The sooner you accept and move toward change, the easier being in tune with your emotional intelligence will be for you.

Your daily goal is still going to be recognizing your emotions, but you are going to take it one step further, Now, I want you to consciously adjust your behavior and actions by placing rational thinking behind your emotions. For example, in a moment that you feel anger, stop and recognize it, but then make sure that your actions are appropriate for the situation. You might be angry, but there is no reason to yell or break things.

Being able to recognize your emotions and then regulate them is what will separate you from the millions of other people out there. While emotions are important to us, nobody wants to be ruled by emotions. You want rational thinking to remain in control here.

Today, I want you to write your goals down in your journal and then go through your day trying to recognize your emotions. When you do, I want you to write down your response to each emotion that you felt and then explain whether you thought it was the right way to react. Don't get too upset if you struggle today. The next few days you're going to keep working at it and on an exercise that will help you regulate your emotions.

Day Seven to Fourteen

"The final forming of a person's character lies in their own hands." - Anne Frank

This next week is going to be full of you using your skills to regulate your behavior. If you struggled with this on day one, then don't worry about it. I will be here to give you some more structure over this next week. As you journal and write down your interactions and your successful and unsuccessful regulation attempts, I also want you to take a look at the emotions you are experiencing. Don't be so focused on regulating them that you become out of touch with your emotions and what they mean to you.

Your goal with regulating your emotions is to be able to respond in the best way in any situation you find yourself in. This could be at work, in an intimate relationship, and even with a friend. You do not want to let your emotions get out of control and then you lose control of a problem. Don't get me wrong, I am not telling you to repress your emotions or hide from them, but rather listen to them and react using rational thinking.

This next week, write down what emotions you felt were harder for you to feel or the ones that you feel like you never felt. Emotions are tricky for us men, and it can take time to get comfortable with truly allowing ourselves to feel them. If you find that you are having trouble with a certain emotion (be that with feeling it or regulating it), then you should take a look at the people around you. Try your best to spot the emotion that you're having difficulty with in them. If you manage to spot someone expressing the emotion, see how they react and write down what you thought about it.

This exercise is important, as it also helps you to begin noticing emotional displays in the people around you. Not only will you be more aware of the emotions of those that you interact with, but you will also be more in tune with your own emotions and have a deeper understanding for how they affect your choices and behavior.

You want to work with the mixed model as you go through this exercise. Remember that it is made of five components, and each of these components is important to have a full and comprehensive panel of abilities. You can also make use of the trait and ability models if you feel more comfortable with those, but you will have more of a complete picture if you look at the mixed model because it is also easy to take it step by step and not overwhelm yourself.

Day Fifteen

"There is only one corner of the universe you can be certain of improving, and that is your own self." - Aldous Huxley

Day fifteen is really a time where you need to take a look at all of your progress. I mean it, you need to sit down this morning and take some time to look at the week in your journal. See where your progress has improved, and how you are becoming more adept at regulating your emotions and being more aware of the emotions of those around you. You need to appreciate the progress that you are making. It can be hard when we do not take a moment to look at our progress. Sometimes, it can feel like you aren't getting anywhere, but that is mainly because you forget where you started and how far you have come.

As always, on the last day of an exercise week I will share with you what my journal looked like. Your journal can look however best suits you, but you should be doing the work of keeping track of your emotional outputs and your responses to them.

"Today my goal is:

- to recognize my emotions

- to regulate my emotional responses with rational thinking

- to be slightly better than I was the day before

- to begin looking towards the emotions that other people feel and experience

- to try and model my responses to what will best fit the emotional climate of the person I am interacting with.

The emotions that I experienced today ranged from:

- happiness - I felt happiness today when I interacted with my wife. She told me some good news about her job and then we went over our children's accomplishments at certain school events. The happiness feeling stayed with me for quite a while and I felt pretty light with my other interactions with people. The rational thought behind my actions was to let them see that I was happy with my interactions and to leave each person with a positive feeling from interacting with me. I smiled a lot, my tone was pleasant, and I maintained gentle eye contact with those around me.

- frustration - during the day I felt frustration rise up and I wanted to get really mad at a situation that I felt was out of my control. I wanted to take time off to go to my child's school event but my boss declined my time off. I had to stop and close my eyes, breathe in and out. Yes, in the moment I felt frustrated, but deeper than that I was feeling sad at possibly disappointing my child. I thought about how to work out a solution and went back to my boss, asking them if I could come in earlier and just leave for a few hours to attend the event then come back to work. My boss agreed to the terms and everyone in the equation would be happy. I felt better knowing that I hadn't acted out in frustration at first and stopped to think about what was really bothering me and then how to deal with it. My problem was disappointing my child, my child wanted me there and was excited about my presence, and my boss wanted me to put in my input and could not spare losing my work for the day. My solution worked out for everyone so that each person got what they wanted at a fair cost.

- relief - As soon as I had my work situation sorted out, relief flooded my body. I felt muscles that I had tensed up release and my brow lines unfurrowed themselves. Soon, I was able to regulate my relief into happy emotional responses and interactions.

*** at this point you should be recognizing that emotions occur on a gradient, so you will be feeling more than just the six basic emotions that we covered in the first week of this journal. I bet that you will be feeling a lot of different emotions and you will be able to recognize each one. That definitely deserves a pat on the back! ***

Interactions that happened today:

- the most important interaction that I experienced today was with my boss. I applied for a day off and he denied me. He was not mean when he denied me and he was not trying to personally attack me, but he was firm that I could not take the day off. At first I was upset then frustrated, but deep down I really felt disappointed that I could not attend my child's school event. I calmed down, rationalized my thinking and then approached my boss with a solution that could fit all of our needs. I realized that my boss's main problem was needing my staffing hours and research and so I made sure that my work would still output my regular workload. Everyone left this interaction happy.

So far in my journey I have been able to recognize my own emotions and then regulate my responses. I have made sure to look at Goleman's mixed model so that I was able to stick to the basics that I have done and make sure that I am making progress towards my future steps in mastering my emotional intelligence."

Days 16-21: Empathy

Day Sixteen to Twenty

"Empathy is about finding echoes of another person in yourself." - Mohsin Hamid

You are halfway through your journey! This is a truly incredible time for you and your emotional intelligence. This next week you will be working on your empathy towards others. Basically, your main goal will be to feel what other people are feeling.

Everyone has emotions that affect them, and when you begin to understand these emotions you can cater your responses so that the other party is more receptive to what you are trying to tell them, or to the message that you are trying to make. You want to understand why they feel the way that they do, if it is a good or bad feeling, and then how you should respond to their emotions. Every single interaction that you have with a person is going to be emotionally charged, but if you put rationale in your decisions then your interactions will be far more successful than in the past.

You can analyze what a person is thinking and feeling, and then deduce why they are acting a certain way. For example, if you feel that your partner is angry and yelling at you, you should be able to get through to the real reason they are acting out, and instead of responding in anger you will work toward responding with rational thought to diffuse the situation.

You have an exercise in empathy for this week, and I want you to record every single day that you practice it. When you are interacting with someone, listen to their story and try to recognize the emotions that they are feeling. Place yourself in their shoes so that you have a better way to connect with them on an empathetic level. In every interaction that you have when you are practicing empathy, ask yourself this question: "What would I want to hear right now if I were feeling how they are?" This should be the question that guides your every response and reaction to others this week. Be present in the moment with the person, don't brush their feelings aside, don't brush them off, and more importantly sometimes all you have to do is listen. You don't have to offer a solution, but simply be there.

Practicing empathy is an important skill that adds to the social skills you need for emotional intelligence. The more empathetic you are, the easier it is to relate to others, form deeper connections, and have more positive interactions.

Day Twenty-One

"If we share our story with someone who responds with empathy and understanding, shame can't survive." - Brene Brown

"My goals this week were to:

- demonstrate empathy by recognizing the emotions of others and responding with the best response that I would want to hear if I were in their shoes

- understand that being empathetic does not always require me to offer a solution, but to understand their emotion

Interactions I had in which I demonstrated empathy and

focused on more than just my own feelings:

- My wife was expressing some concerns regarding one of our children's grades. She seemed frustrated and upset, But I was not sure what solution I could really offer her. I sat in silence for a minute and let her talk about what was eating at her regarding our child's school performance and I gathered that she was feeling like she was failing our child herself. This was about more than just his school performance, but her performance as a mother. At first, I listened to what my wife was saying and I let her vent. Then, when I realized that her feelings were internalized at herself I aimed to comfort her. I know that in this situation I would not want someone to ridicule my child's grades because that would make me feel like more of a failure. Instead, once she was calm I held her, reassured her that she was doing the best that she could and then I came up with a plan with her so that she and I could help our child raise their grades, or perhaps just find out the reason for the grades slipping."

Days 22-30: Influence

"Leadership is influence." - John C. Maxwell

You have made it almost a month into this incredible journey and I am so proud of how far your emotional intelligence has come. As a man, it takes big steps to even start trying to understand your emotions, accept your emotions, and then communicate these emotions to the people around you. If you have taken just one step towards trying to understand your emotions, then that deserves recognition.

Please remember that mastering your emotional intelligence is not a one day process; sometimes it is not even a one month process! It can take time, and you might have to spend more time on certain exercises before you feel completely ready to move onto the next one. That is completely okay, so do not feel like you have let yourself down, and do not be overly hard on yourself. This takes time. It is better to make sure you are being true to yourself versus rushing through this journey. There is also nothing stopping you from doing this journey again and again. Keep working it, keep improving on your ability to empathize and your ability to accept your own emotions, and then respond with rational thinking. There are endless possibilities in this world for you to practice on your emotional intelligence.

As you come into this last week of this journaling experience, our focus is going to shift into working on an entire and complete picture. Instead of working on just one area, you are going to work on recognizing your emotions, understanding your own emotions and where they are stemming from, as well as work on recognizing and empathizing with the emotions of the people that you interact with.

So, let us map this out in goals for our journal:

- Recognize my own emotions and handle them with rational thought

- Recognize the emotions of others and empathize with their feelings

- Navigate and use my emotional intelligence to create favorable social situations

There are two things that you will be working on during this week: your influence as well as your motivation.

Exercise one involves your influence during a social situation. When you are in any social interaction this week (remember to take it one day at a time), try using your influence on a social situation to your benefit. This means being honest and open about your own emotions and empathize with theirs. You will create an even playing field and the person you are interacting with will be more likely to hear your side of a story and agree to a course of action that you have planned.

Exercise two for the week (and yes, you will be working on each exercise each day of this week) involves your motivation. Without motivation, we get nowhere. As you work on understanding emotions this week, focus on why you want to increase your emotional intelligence. Focus on your goals. It helps if you have something that you are passionate about that you want to reach in order to motivate you to further analyze emotions. Keep track of your motivation. When you find yourself becoming unmotivated, pull out your journal and make a list of all the reasons that you should feel motivated. For example, I had a friend who was just starting this course out and they always struggled with feeling angry or sad. Their motivation came with the need to understand their emotions and strive to attain happier and more consistently healthy and positive emotions.

In your journal I also want you to write down about how you practiced listening each day. Remember, sometimes all the work you need to do is to listen to someone else and that meets all their needs. However, you do need to be an active listener. Take this excerpt from my journal on day twenty-five:

"Today I had the opportunity to really practice my listening skills when my daughter came up to me and wanted to discuss a situation at her school. Normally she goes to her mother with these things, but for some reason she decided to entrust her story with me. This is a pivotal moment in our communication and if I handled it the right way then I know that I solidified a bond with my daughter. All I had to do was listen to her. Not just nod my head, or dismiss her story, but actively listen to what she had to tell me, what she wanted to say to me. When I was listening to her story I asked questions about her feelings, or questions that prompted her to go more in depth with her story. Then, I repeated what she said back to me at certain intervals to show her that I was truly engaged in her story."

The outcome of that situation was that my daughter now comes to talk to me about a lot more things, and I treasure the foundation that we have built simply through active listening.

Listen to your emotions, don't shy away from them. Remember that negative emotions can be expressed positively. If you are angry at a work situation or even in your private family life, you do not have to express yourself in a negative manner. By now I am sure you have that point drilled into your head. I wish you luck as you continue through your journey and I hope this journal has helped you. I find that going through my journal every now and then helps cement the foundation that I have built my emotional intelligence on, so you might want to keep your journal around you even when you have finished this journey!

Conclusion

Wow! This has surely been an incredible journey for you to go through. I want to start off by saying thank you for choosing this book and thank you for sticking through the guide and putting in the work to master your emotional intelligence. Mastering your emotional intelligence is no small feat, and you should be proud of yourself for coming this far.

I want you to remember that you can and should keep working on and practicing your emotional intelligence! It is like a muscle that you need to keep healthy and exercised. Don't make the mistake of becoming too cocky and self-assured and forgetting to control your own emotions or lose your ability to empathize with those around you.

My goal for you is that by now you have an understanding of your emotions. However, I really want more than just that for you. I want you to also understand the emotions of others and to be able to navigate their emotions so that you have successful social interactions. Emotional intelligence is an amazing ability to understand yourself and those around you. There is nothing else that will give you such insight into human behavior as understanding their emotions.

In chapter one you learned all about what the basic emotions were. Remember that these are important emotions to understand, but that they do not make the emotional range. Emotions occur on a gradient, and they can vary from person to person based on cultural experiences as well. The most important part about experiencing our emotions is learning how to embrace them and fully embrace our feelings. Don't hide behind anger and pride because it is easier than confronting your other emotions.

As men, it can be easy to be fooled by our emotions. This is because most of the time we are not adjusted to understanding and handling our emotions the same way that women are. Our society has conditioned us to believe that anything more than anger or pride makes us less of a man. However, that is not the truth. You are not less of a man because you feel. Being in tune with your emotions makes it so that you are that much more of a man. You are complete when you have mastered your emotional intelligence, because then you are at the top of your game. Every single decision that we make is based on emotion, not logic — as much as we try to convince ourselves otherwise. The goal is to understand your emotions and use rational reasoning to make your decisions.

In chapter two the EQ models were discussed, and while we learned that there were three different models, our area of focus was Daniel Goleman's mixed model. The mixed model is based off of five components: your self-awareness, self-regulation, motivation, empathy, and social skills. All of these components are necessary to understand and implement in your reasoning so that you are able to be emotionally aware and emotionally mature. You can make use of all of the models, but study the mixed model the most because this is the most universal model when it comes to conquering your emotional intelligence.

As you have cycled through emotions, you have probably learned by now that being self-aware is the first step to truly getting anywhere when it comes to emotions. Learning how to be self-aware will help you learn how to evaluate what emotions you are feeling in each moment. When you recognize your emotions and feelings, then you stand a better chance at navigating your response to outside stimuli. It is also one of the first steps towards evaluating the emotions of others.

When you are self-aware, then you can self-regulate! This is an amazing step that shows you are making progress. Self-regulation means that you are able to manage your emotions. This means that simply because you are angry, that does not mean you act in inappropriate ways. You know how to navigate your emotions to make the right social choices. You are able to motivate yourself as well and keep yourself on track. Emotional intelligence is not a one step solution to the world's problems, but it can certainly help alleviate the problems in your personal life.

Finally, you should also be able to interpret through social cues how people feel and go through emotions. Through your daily interactions, you and the people you are interacting with go through a hundred different feelings and emotions. Your interactions will go smoother when you are able to identify their emotions and rationalize your responses in accordance to what will best fit the social situation. It all ties in together, and it all needs to be there in order to work for your best benefit. You cannot have one quality without the other, otherwise your emotional intelligence picture is not complete.

I hope that you enjoyed taking the thirty day plan and making it work for you! I enjoyed making it, and it was designed to give you the best possible ability to succeed in this world. Remember that it does not have to only be thirty days. You can extend the program and work on it every single day for as long as you choose to. If you find that you are struggling in one particular area, then you should not hesitate to repeat the steps that you need some extra work in. There is never shame in making sure that you have all of your emotional intelligence skills sharpened and ready for use.

I have done my part. I have illustrated what emotional

intelligence is, how it works, and how you can make it work to your best advantage. I have even included a thirty day plan that is designed to help you boost your emotional intelligence further than where it currently sits. There is a solution to every problem that you encounter, and I am glad that I can offer up this solution to you. This does not have to be hard or trying on your patience. Simply take it one step at a time, and I am confident that by the end you will have mastered your emotions and raised your social awareness of others' emotions. In short, I know you've got this!

There will be an audiobook coming out soon that you should be on the lookout for. Like this book, it is geared toward men who are often overlooked in this market. The audiobook is based on affirmations and included guided meditation techniques and hypnosis that helps reprogram men who have a harder time being honest about their true emotions. There is a lot of fascinating information out in the world that will help you be your best and strongest self - both emotionally and mentally.

I want to give you a final thank you and good-bye as this book comes to a close, but this does not mean that your journey has to end here. I have faith and confidence in you.

Dear Reader,

As an independent author,
   and one-man operation
   - my marketing budget is next to zero.

As such, the only way
   I can get my books in-front of valued customers
   is with reviews.

Unfortunately, I'm competing against authors and
   giant publishing companies
   with multi-million-dollar marketing teams.

These behemoths can afford
   to give away hundreds of free books
   to boost their ranking and success.

Which as much as I'd love to –
   I simply can't afford to do.

That's why your honest review
   will not only be invaluable to me,
   but also to other readers on Amazon.

Yours sincerely,

John Adams

References

Brogaard, B. (2018). Basic and Complex Emotions. Retrieved from https://www.psychologytoday.com/us/blog/the-superhuman-mind/201806/basic-and-complex-emotions

Burton, N. (2015). Empathy Vs Sympathy. Retrieved from https://www.psychologytoday.com/us/blog/hide-and-seek/201505/empathy-vs-sympathy

Chang, PHD, L. (2019). Retrieved from https://www.mindfulnessmuse.com/dialectical-behavior-therapy/recognize-your-emotions-in-6-steps

Cherry, K. (2019). How to Read Body Language and Facial Expressions. Retrieved from https://www.verywellmind.com/understand-body-language-and-facial-expressions-4147228

Cherry, K. (2019). The 6 Types of Basic Emotions and Their Effect on Human Behavior. Retrieved from https://www.verywellmind.com/an-overview-of-the-types-of-emotions-4163976

Cherry, K. (2019). 5 Key Components of Emotional Intelligence. Retrieved from https://www.verywellmind.com/components-of-emotional-intelligence-2795438

Deutschendorf, H. (2019). Why Emotionally Intelligent People Are More Successful. Retrieved from https://www.fastcompany.com/3047455/why-emotionally-intelligent-people-are-more-successful

Freedman, J. (2019). Emotional Intelligence and Your Career:

EQ for Talent Infographic. Retrieved from https://www.6seconds.org/2014/04/12/emotional-intelligence-career/

Fitzgerald, V. (2016). HuffPost is now a part of Oath. Retrieved from https://www.huffpost.com/entry/2-phrases-men-are-afraid-to-say-to-our-partners_b_5790d103e4b0a86259d0d6a6

Goleman, D. (2019). Emotional Intelligence - Daniel Goleman. Retrieved from http://www.danielgoleman.info/topics/emotional-intelligence/

Harra, Dr, C. (2013). 6 Tips For Holding It Together. Retrieved from https://www.huffpost.com/entry/controlling-your-emotions_b_3654326?guce_referrer=aHR0cHM6Ly93d3cuZ29vZ2xlLm5sLw&guce_referrer_sig=AQAAAE2VJ5HpWx-6XCz0tiKcGOF2Nmx0wQ8A_tqNoasbtR9Ui7YwrlIVb1dKZfjBKyuzbR7grv0py4u90RH5WWWLhGiS3yGpTlmynhiI90-4UR_cDMZvEDLntivfN8ubrqZPVSHFJjz32FeUStcI32BDwiFWMee_0RIyQqgmaDPd3TWY&guccounter=2

Helpful vs Harmful: Ways to Manage Emotions. (2019). Retrieved from http://www.mentalhealthamerica.net/conditions/helpful-vs-harmful-ways-manage-emotions

Krauss Whitbourne, S. (2015). 5 Ways to Get Your Unwanted Emotions Under Control. Retrieved from https://www.psychologytoday.com/intl/blog/fulfillment-any-age/201502/5-ways-get-your-unwanted-emotions-under-control

Managing Your Emotions at Work: Controlling Your Feelings... Before They Control You. (2019). Retrieved from https://www.mindtools.com/pages/article/newCDV_41.htm

Schmitz, T. (2016). Empathy - Responding to Others | The Conover Company. Retrieved from https://www.conovercompany.com/empathy-responding-to-others/

Simons, I. (2009). Why Do We Have Emotions?. Retrieved from https://www.psychologytoday.com/us/blog/the-literary-mind/200911/why-do-we-have-emotions

The 3 Models. (2019). Retrieved from http://theimportanceofemotionalintelligence.weebly.com/the-3-models.html

CPSIA information can be obtained
at www.ICGtesting.com
Printed in the USA
LVHW081426120922
728165LV00005B/152